VOGUE ON
GIANNI VERSACE

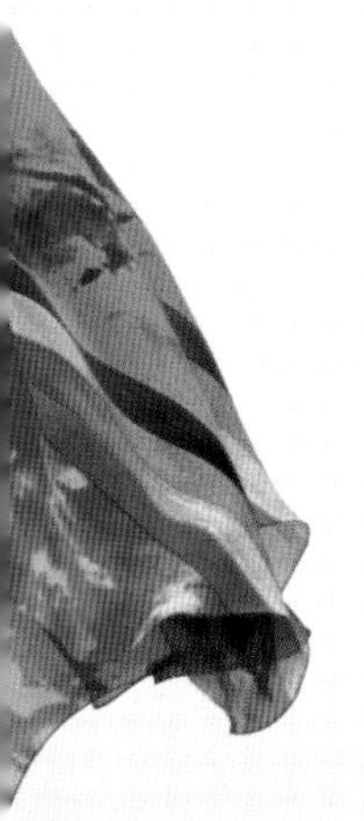

Charlotte Sinclair

QUADRILLE

The Versace Collective: a glamour-dazzle of supermodels dressed by – and with – the man himself. Photograph by Vittorio Rastelli.

page 1 *Linda Evangelista photographed by Patrick Demarchelier in a Versace strapless and rhinestone-garnished silk crêpe dress worn with a billowing taffeta opera coat.*

pages 2-3 *A crêpe-de-chine flared jumpsuit in a distinctively Versace vibrant print. Photograph by Andrew Macpherson.*

'VOGUE'S MAIN INGREDIENTS ARE INTELLIGENCE, IMAGINATION, HUMOUR, AND A HINT OF SNOBBISHNESS THAT I HAVE ALWAYS LOVED...'

GIANNI VERSACE

THE DRESSMAKER'S SON

'Any good portrait of Gianni Versace will reveal the lofty brow and thoughtful eyes, the melancholy mouth in its neat thicket of square-clipped bead', described *Vogue*, introducing the designer whose accomplished collections had by 1985 already marked him as one of the most exciting names in fashion. With the article was the portrait in question: a photograph by Bert Stern in which Versace's face is half-shadowed behind a classical pillar, a symbolic nod towards the Greek and Roman classicism that was Versace's inspiration and design hallmark. 'What cannot be shown in a photograph,' the magazine continued, 'is his unexpectedly gentle manner. Unlike many highly successful creative designers, he is shy. Ask him to talk about himself and he says, "You will find me in my work."'

Versace said of himself 'You will find me in my work.' His debut portrait for Vogue, *taken by Bert Stern in 1985, reveals this self-effacing side of the master showman.*

Overleaf *Helena Christensen in a show-stopping silk grosgrain dress with crown-jewelled bodice and a theatrical scene printed on the underside of the cascading train. Photograph by Patrick Demarchelier.*

For all his declared modesty, Versace gazed from his portrait in a manner more direct than self-effacing. As *Vogue* commented, 'There is nothing diffident about his work: it has always been remarkable for its self-assurance and adventurousness.' During almost twenty years at the head of his house, Versace's fashions became an expression of pure Italian glamour, a celebration of life lived large – that is, *à la* Versace. His clothes described an easy, moneyed existence, a life of flitting from palazzo to private plane, of delicate, silvery chain-mail evening dresses worn by the light of a disco ball or paparazzi flash. A notion of vampish womanhood much inspired by his younger sister, Donatella, a blonde, tanned, diamond-dripping spitfire who was his muse, accomplice and an essential component in the success of his house and its attendant glamour. Donatella, *Vogue* wrote a year after Gianni's death, 'pushed him in the headline-grabbing direction that ultimately made him one of the world's most famous designers'.

Versace was a star, and his clothes were made for stars; few other designers of his era cultivated or enjoyed such a close, mutually beneficial relationship with celebrity, one that played out in newspapers and magazines around the world and in the audiences of his catwalk shows, altering fashion's rapport with mass culture.

‘YOU WEAR VERSACE: YOU BELIEVE IN DARING AND DRAMA.’

ANDRÉ LEON TALLEY

Style, as Versace proved, was no longer for the elite. Yet even Madonna was overawed by the Versace lifestyle. He lived as a Renaissance prince, in palaces of extraordinary luxury, his world a reflection of his fashions. These were clothes as attitude. To wear Versace (according to *American Vogue*'s André Leon Talley) was to 'believe in daring and drama.' 'Who wears Versace?' inquired *Vogue* in 1985. 'These clothes are not for shrinking violets.'

No, indeed. Versace's concept of slinky femininity was specific but infinitely adaptable, spanning couture, daywear, homeware, accessories, perfume and cosmetics, a strategy that ensured the company's global success and a multi-million dollar empire while offering a little Versace magic for every price point. This was a designer for the age, who dressed a woman's life from the boardroom to the bedroom and back again, in a body-conscious, often brazen style that distilled the cultural preoccupations of the eighties and nineties, the era of the power woman and power suit, the supermodel and celebrity. A decade after his death, *Vogue* wrote, 'Versace defined late twentieth-century glamour, invented the supermodel and sanctioned in the public consciousness a supremely self-assured feminine sexuality.'

Yet this same unflinching sensuality, as expressed in Versace's assimilation of the risqué and potentially risible – including bondage and pop-culture kitsch – along with his profligate use of embellishment, pattern, colour and ornament, and daring cut (career-altering, in the case of Elizabeth Hurley), frequently attracted charges of vulgarity. When he showed denim on his couture catwalk it caused a small, violent thrill to pass through the grey houses of Paris fashion. Versace's insignia, a golden, snake-haired Medusa, was symbolic of a sensibility that was 'at once classical, alluring, theatrical, garish and dangerous,' wrote the fashion historian Deborah Ball. But this notion of Versace – walking the tightrope between good taste and bad – was only ever half the story. Convention, the designer believed, was meant to be subverted: 'You have to know it to then ignore it, you have to love it to then abandon it and, translating it, make it become tradition again, to then once again betray it.' In photographs of Linda

Mixing denim and a Rococo-print full silk skirt, Versace combined scuffed cowboy charm with the high court of Versailles in inimitable style. Photograph by Tyen.

Evangelista, Christy Turlington, Kate Moss – captured by Herb Ritts, Bruce Weber, Horst and Mario Testino – *Vogue* revealed Versace's sure instinct for how women wanted to dress. The magazine disclosed his discipline and deft intelligence, exquisite workmanship and technical verve; his innovative use of materials and respect for Italy's traditions of artisanship.

Stephanie Seymour photographed in 1990 by Herb Ritts, wearing a flying, feathered Versace catsuit. A perfect showcase for the conspicuous sensuality that was the designer's hallmark.

Overleaf *Naomi Campbell demonstrates the Versace approach to suiting (left) – short, tight, tomato-red, and miles of bare, well-turned legs. Photograph by Albert Watson. Linda Evangelista models a daring evening dress (right) of intricate surface detail. Photograph by Nick Knight.*

By the time of his brutal murder in 1997, the designer had altered the fashion vocabulary to create a style that was unquestionably Versace, a signature that would guarantee his legacy. So, too, had he altered the fashion business; *The New York Times* described it as 'an industry now driven by contemporary culture because Mr. Versace made it that way.' If the Versace name had come to stand for an outsized and conspicuous brand of glamour, it also expressed the renewed dominance of Italian design, and a sense of quality and unassailable luxury. 'I like to be different,' he told *Vogue* in 1985. 'I like to break barriers. It's a game I play with myself – all the time I push myself into doing something new.'

Gianni Versace was born on 2 December 1946, in Reggio di Calabria, a port in the far south of Italy facing Sicily over the Strait of Messina. Enclosed by mountains, Reggio is a place much tormented by disasters both natural and manmade: the town has suffered floods, droughts and earthquakes, while 70% of its buildings were bombed during the Second World War. Its populace, rough-hewn mountain people, lived in isolated poverty until as recently as 1963 when a highway was built, connecting the town to civilization. Even today the area is still under the sway of the powerful Calabrian mafia, the 'Ndrangheta.

Versace was one of three children born to Nino and Franca Versace, the middle child between older brother, Santo, and younger sister, Donatella. His father was a salesman, while his mother ran a successful dress shop – 'she could cut cloth for a new dress without following a pattern, using just pins to mark the edges,' reported Deborah Ball.

As a child, Gianni spent his afternoons in his mother's atelier, playing with scraps of material and being endlessly fussed over by the seamstresses who occupied the shop. He later said, 'My life was like a Fellini film, I grew up surrounded by all women. I was spoiled. I had twenty girlfriends and twenty mothers.' As Vogue disclosed in 1980, 'His mother's was the best couture house: as a child he could watch from the terrace as the customers arrived, then he would run down to the atelier to make sketches and watch the fittings. Versace is in fact one of the few fashion designers who can make a dress, cut and sew.' Even then he understood how women wanted to dress. He informed *The New Yorker* in 1994, 'All the women come in, and first I look at the women. I never look at the clothing she wear. I try to understand the way she move, the way she is, and I try to give advice to her – I was fourteen years old. And these women trusted me. My mother's atelier, it was like a school.' It was there, he said, 'I learnt the way to cut.'

The young Versace sought out ever 'more beautiful and extraordinary' beads, crystals and braids to use in his mother's atelier. The formative experience developed his love for embellishment, seen here in a Herb Ritts close-up of a jewelled bodysuit.

Versace's experience of watching his mother in her atelier (a woman who genuflected before beginning cutting) was to be of lasting impact. As he wrote in his book, *Signatures*, 'A black velvet dress is my earliest memory. I thought: "Now my mother will shorten it in front, leave it longer in the back, and then do something about the rules, something daring." This is precisely what happened. Even thought I was so young (I was around nine), something was already inside me: in reality, that fitting has never ended. That black dress is always there, elegant, stately, the first that I remember.' Equally formative were the trips the young Versace made to Messina to help his mother select extra embellishments for her embroidery. He wrote, 'I took the ferry, and each time I tried to choose more beautiful and extraordinary materials.' Delivering this glittering haul of stones, beads, crystals and braid to his mother's seamstress, Maria, a woman 'with something magic about her hands', he described the 'Reliefs, openwork, arabesques [that] came to life and grew between her fingers, while pearls, jet, drops and crystals were there transformed into waves, waterfalls, flowers, leaves, and precious bas-reliefs.'

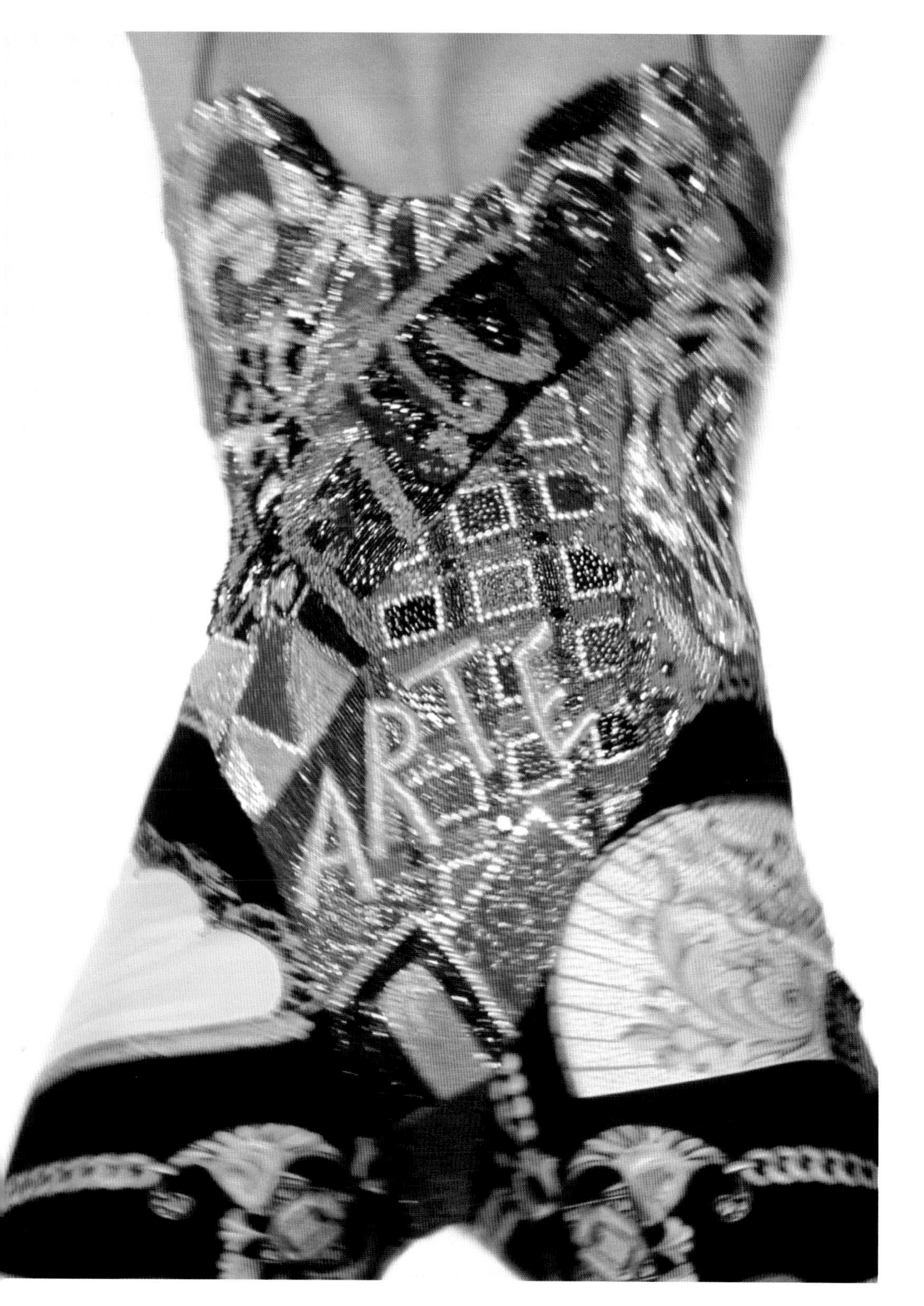

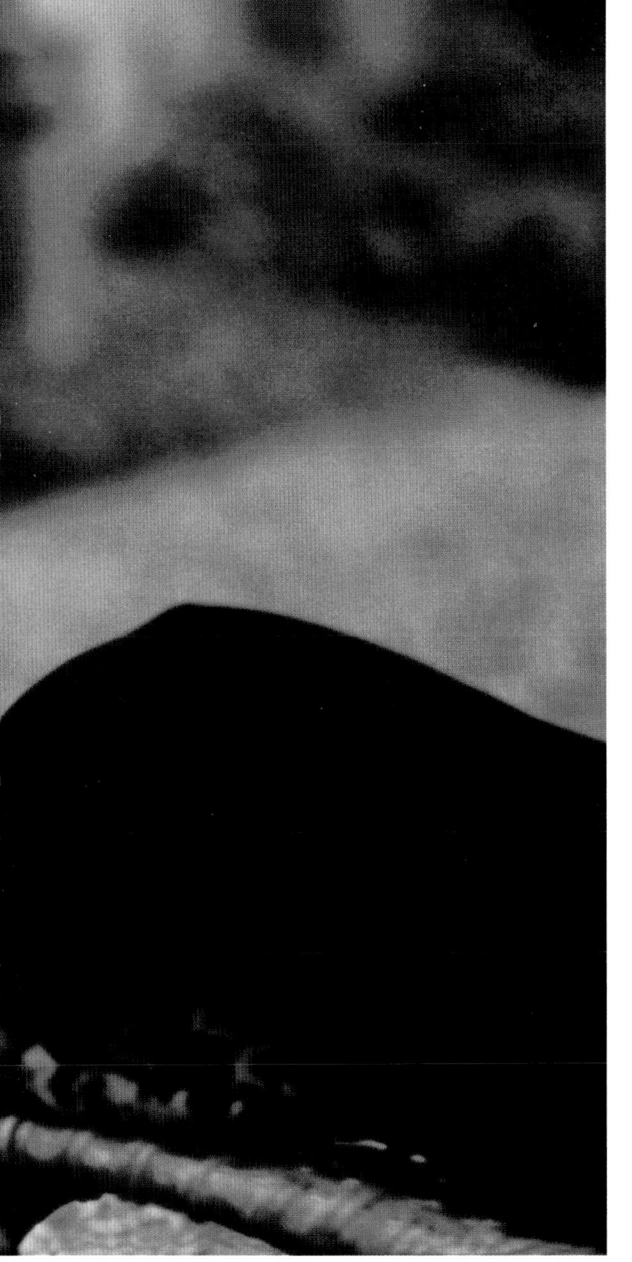

'VERSACE DEFINED LATE TWENTIETH-CENTURY GLAMOUR.'

VOGUE

Versace's designs communicated the bold-faced allure and conspicuous luxury of the eighties. These notions are deftly referenced with a rhinestone-sprinkled sleeve on a Dynasty*-worthy black velvet dress, photographed by Neil Kirk.*

Versace's love of surface detail, of fine work and embellishment was born in these moments.

Reggio's past extended an equally powerful influence on the young Versace. 'His love for the classical has been with him since the day when, as a small boy, he used to play football with his friends in a ruined Greek temple on a beach in southern Italy,' *Vogue* reported in 1985. 'He spent the first above-subsistence money he ever earned on pieces of sculpture.' In aggrandising fashion, Versace later wrote, 'I come from a land with a rich history, from Magna Graecia, full of vivacity. Its roots are old, ancient roots that knew the aristocracy of sculptural draperies; from there comes the force to dare, the will to outdo myself, the stimulus to give even more.'

Versace, in whose life and designs high and low culture were vigorously mixed, found a source of both in Reggio. Donatella became Gianni's companion on nightly escapades. As *Vogue* reported in 1998, from a young age 'Donatella and Gianni were stealing the keys to their father's car and sneaking into discos. At eleven Donatella was already dyeing her hair – "just the front bits, and the streaks got bigger and bigger" – and wearing the outrageous outfits her big brother, ten years her senior, designed for her. "You can't imagine how much Gianni spoiled me," she laughs. "He made me naughty. Those clothes he designed for me, they weren't at all like my mother's elegant taste." ' Gianni told *Vogue* in 1990, 'I would go out every night, dreaming to be a rock musician.' Donatella added, 'I was always into fashion as a little girl, always something very aggressive. We always had the same taste and had so much fun. Everything that was forbidden, I could do with Gianni.'

Good in bed: Versace's irresistible, candy-pink, curve-hugging dress broadcasts an irrepressible, kittenish sexuality. Photograph by Ellen von Unwerth.

The increasingly blonde Donatella was to become Gianni's muse and provocateur, embodying his vision of femininity. *Vogue* reported, 'The story he loved to tell about being marched past the local brothel every day with his mother's hands clamped over his eyes may well have been apocryphal but certainly something sparked a Madonna/whore fixation in him.' Even as a child, Versace had a fixed idea of womanhood, filling his school notebooks with sketches of women with the va-va-voom dimensions of Sophia Loren. 'Those sketches were a sign of what I would become,' he said. Though his father pushed Gianni to study surveying, his mother, recognising her son's fascination for design and complete lack of enthusiasm for academia, opened a fashion boutique in 1965 and made Gianni head buyer. Free to stock whichever designers he chose, Gianni attended shows in Florence and Paris, proving himself adept at anticipating the looks which would sell best to his *alta borghesia* (upper-middle class) customers.

It was a dynamic time in Italian fashion. In the fifties, supported by renewed growth in Italy's textile industries from Como silk to Tuscan leather, Italian designers such as Pucci, Simonetta and Schuberth appealed to the burgeoning American casual market. So too the notion of Italy as the source of *la dolce vita*, a glamorous, sunny, carefree lifestyle with a wardrobe of capri pants, beach outfits and print cotton dresses to match. The appellation 'Made In Italy' became a universal signifier of quality, much burnished by the appearance of Hollywood stars, such as Elizabeth Taylor and Audrey Hepburn, wearing Italian designs during breaks from filming at the famous Cinecittà studios. By the sixties and early seventies – the age of Biba, the miniskirt, and Woodstock – the concept of ready-to-wear had exploded in popularity, and Italy's textile factories, with their equal focus on style, material and quality of manufacture, had pushed the country to the forefront of a revolution in design.

Made in Italy: Versace's early success capitalised on Italian ready-to-wear's growth in popularity and global dominance, with its myriad price points, from socks to suits. Here, a swimsuit and handbag are given the Versace treatment in bold prints. Photograph by Tyen.

While Versace attended the twice-yearly fashion shows, eyeing the latest collections for items to buy for his mother's boutique, he nurtured ambitions for his own career in design. He began taking along his sketch portfolio to drum up interest and, in 1972, succeeded in catching the eye of the owner of Florentine Flowers, a clothing manufacturer in Lucca. (Santo Versace, by now a trained accountant, negotiated a contract on his behalf: the first of many.) The unknown, untested twenty-five year old completed a single collection for Florentine Flowers – which, as *Vogue* reported, 'sold immediately'

and with such success that the company bought Versace a Volkswagen convertible – before quitting for Milan, Italy's newly appointed fashion capital. In 1973 he was signed to the Girombelli group and charged with creating youthful collections for their Genny and Complice labels, and soon after, for Callaghan, the firm that discovered Romeo Gigli.

Supplying his teams of assistants with his sketches, visiting the factories to negotiate his exacting vision for a textile, then draping, pinning and cutting garments into shape on a mannequin or fit model in the studio – his distinct method of working – Versace quickly became known for his attention to detail and his indefatigable work ethic and, in his clothes, a contemporary, relaxed look defined by deft cut and luxurious fabrics. *Vogue* Paris reported of his designs for Callaghan: 'Unknown just three years ago, he is one of the designers that people are talking most about.' A 1976 fashion spread in *Vogue* highlighted 'Genny's shirt jacket and pants in olive wool gabardine', showing three ways to wear Versace's tailored separates. An illustration from the same year showed a white tunic, a 'slip of a dress with splits over iced blue dress by Gianni Versace for Genny' – 'Note, the finely tailored detail'.

A 1976 sketch in Vogue *shows a hyacinth-blue lettuce-edged silky jersey tunic, part of Versace's early collections for Genny.*

Overleaf *A 1988 black leather bomber jacket with a fur collar by Versace showed the designer's dexterity with the sexy, supple and deliciously luxuriant material that was a hallmark of his collections. Photograph by Alex Chatelain.*

Versace's method of designing onto the dimensions of a woman's body caught the eye of legendary fashion editor Diana Vreeland. In his book, *Signatures*, Versace described her backstage in 1977: 'It was a simple show, the only charm being enormous sashes to drape around the waist, on the hips, or under the chest of the girls. Thus before every exit I had to work in a great rush, trying to be as imaginative and quick as possible. She was always there, watching me with her scrutinizing and penetrating eyes, but early on, carried away by my work, I forgot she was there.' At the end of the show she embraced Versace, and said, 'I have never seen anyone drape a dress so well and in such little time.' He gave her a pair of leather trousers and a white blouse. 'When she later sent me a photograph of herself wearing the pants and shirt in her unmistakable style,' he wrote. 'I was enchanted and decided that one must never believe that an older woman cannot wear certain things.

‘LEATHER …
ONE OF THE
MATERIALS
I PREFER.’

GIANNI VERSACE

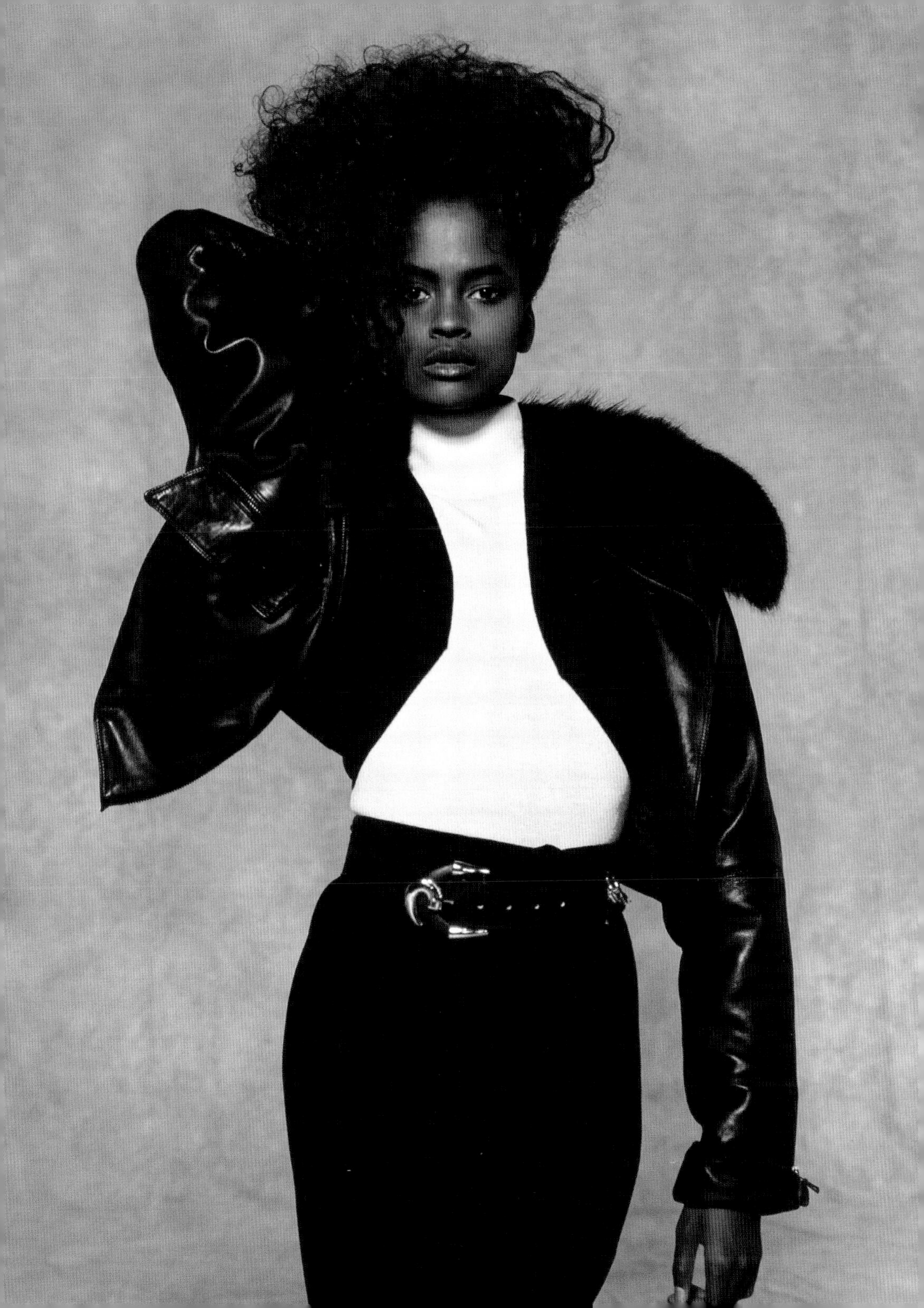

This memory led me to an even greater love of leather, which remains one of the materials I prefer.'

Already the fabric had become a Versace signature. As he told *Interview* magazine, 'I think the first time I sensed the key to my style was in 1976, when I did a collection combining lots of leather with silk. No one had shown an entire collection in leather or other hard materials before, with the desired effect being elegance and class.' The seventies were a process of distillation for Versace. As he wrote, 'It was during that period that the first contrasts appeared in my fashions, later becoming the key to all my creations. That reference to the past mixed with the present, that antithesis in the pairing of furs and silk, which came to me spontaneously in those years, expressed the desire for a double vision in all things: an elegant and traditional face and an avant-garde face, the face of the past and that of the future.'

By 1978, Versace was a commercial success, his various collections – and contracts negotiated by his brother – earning him thousands of lire every month and a growing reputation for his talent. Yet it wasn't enough to satisfy Gianni's ambitions. He had jealously observed the success of his contemporary, Giorgio Armani, who had launched his eponymous line in 1974, and longed to design under his own name. Gianni and Santo began working on a business plan for his own house and together found a site for the first Versace boutique, on Milan's smart Via della Spiga. With Donatella and Santo by his side, the house of Versace was born on 28 March 1978 with a show at Milan's Palazzo della Permanente. The collection, including simple shirt-dresses tied at the waist with silk scarves, received a muted response but was enough to get him noticed. A few months later, *Vogue* featured the first outfits under his own label, including a form-fitting brown leather coat, worn with a fox fur slung over the model's shoulder. The clothes radiated confidence and sensuality; so too the model who glowered from the photographs. The emblems of Versace style – sex, money, luxury – were already working a powerful seduction.

A pair of knife-sharp coats by Versace in pleated, khaki wool and brown leather reveal the designer's instinct for texture and cut. Photograph by Lothar Schmid.

'THOSE WHO FALL IN LOVE WITH THE MEDUSA HAVE NO WAY BACK.'

GIANNI VERSACE

Accounts differ on how Versace struck upon a Greek mythological monster for his house insignia. According to the designer, it was inspired by the ancient mosaic floors and ruins he played amongst as a child. Fashion historian Deborah Ball reported that the choice was more accidental: the designer discovered a Medusa carved into the doorknocker of the grand Milanese palazzo he bought in 1981. Either way, it was a highly effective cipher for Versace's burgeoning success. As the designer himself attested, 'those who fall in love with the Medusa have no way back. So why not imagine that those whom Versace conquers – that they, too cannot go back?'

Versace swiftly conquered the fashion landscape. Within months of his debut, the Versace name had become synonymous with *la moda italiana*: a combination of luxury and bold attitude for which there was a worldwide appetite in the late seventies. Free from the flash and clash that later became his byword, Versace's early collections were distinct for their focus on draping, pleating, tailoring and technique. They were directly inspired by French couturiers Vionnet and Madame Grès, yet with a recognisably Italian – recognisably Versace – sensuality of cut. As the former editor of *Vogue* Paris, Joan Juliet Buck, said, Versace's debut work was 'skittish and sexy and immediately comprehensible.' Reviewing the collections in 1979, *Vogue* declared, 'Italy is Gianni Versace's black and blue leather kimonos with silk and suede. It is strange compelling colours, lush prints. Soft as soft can be. And no jewels.' His designs featured harem pants in delicate, printed silk, and jumpsuits slashed to the navel worn with leather obi belts. These were modelled to compelling effect by Iman, Kelly LeBrock and Jerry Hall in Versace's advertising campaigns, in which expensive, big name female models (and their male counterparts) were photographed *en masse*, splayed across a bed of satin pillows in what resembled a post-coital puddle. These glossy, decadently sexy pictures were the work of fashion photographer Richard Avedon, who, from 1979 onwards, produced the marketing images that delivered a definitive notion of Versace glamour.

In 1979, Vogue *featured this 'black leather shapely kimono, wide raglan sleeves, narrow wrists, belted over a jungle of olive printed chiffon.' Photograph by François Lamy.*

Overleaf *'Compelling colour' – a bright pink leather obi belt worn over a jumpsuit slashed below the waist. Photograph by Albert Watson.*

‘SKITTISH
AND SEXY AND
IMMEDIATELY
COMPREHENSIBLE.’

JOAN JULIET BUCK

'GOOD FASHION IS PURE FORM. NOT COMPLICATED.'

GIANNI VERSACE

Photographer Bruce Weber captures luxury-minded Versace daywear: a voluminous cream overcoat worn, by bicycle, over suede jodhpurs.

Previous pages *A seemingly demure dress is made startlingly sexy with a vertebrae-exposing draped back and thigh-high slash (left). Photograph by Michel Arnaud.*
'The first rule of sex appeal,' writes Vogue, *'reveal, then conceal.' Executed perfectly by Versace in a column of provocatively sliced black silk (right). Photograph by Kim Knott.*

With their daring, sheer layers and attention-catching beading and brocade, Versace's early work hinted at his later output, not least in its preoccupation with revealing and glorifying the shape of a woman's body. These were clothes that courted the male gaze, to notice, and be noticed in. His audacious thigh-split gowns and backless bodices were beautifully constructed and never unflattering. Versace could tailor a garment to conceal problem areas while emphasising what he saw as a woman's best features: her décolletage, her back, her waist. As features writer Vicki Woods said, 'His clothes were quite traditional. They curve out at the bosom, in at the waist, and out again over the hips.'

When it came to daywear, Versace's clothes borrowed a sense of ease from menswear – without sacrificing their feminine silhouette. (Alongside women's fashions, Versace launched his menswear line in September 1978.) For *Vogue*, Bruce Weber photographed the designer's sell-out leather jodhpurs and cashmere coats on models on bicycles or striding with purpose along the British coastline. Simultaneously, Versace was developing his feeling for colour and print and an interest in art that was to become a hallmark of his designs. The caption for a 1982 *Vogue* sketch described a heady concoction: 'Wrap-over double-layered silk chiffon sarong, short at the front, long at the back, art deco design with beads, bright blocks of blue stripes, lemon.'

His eveningwear was immediately desirable. A September 1985 *Vogue* spread photographed by Herb Ritts showed a model, on one page a close-up of her head and shoulders, the other of her waist and ankles, the better to reveal the texture of Versace's 'molten silver sarong and vest with black beaded leather jacket', an outfit of extraordinary detail: thousands of silver bugle beads sewn in long, lateral lines, broken up with deco circles, the leather jacket cut on the hip and with an oversized pointed collar worked with yet more bugle beads.

Luxuriant leather looks dominated *Vogue's* Versace coverage of the early eighties, including body-conscious coats trimmed with fox fur and form-fitting trousers. But, as he later said, 'Under the leather coats, there were soft jersey dresses, which people don't remember.' *Vogue* wrote of the designer, 'the unmistakable bloom of luxury which rests on every Versace garment comes from the way he uses fabrics. His *nonchalance de luxe* is best demonstrated in extravagant combinations of leather, metal, silk and cashmere. He uses velvet and corduroy with equal abandon – nor does he use them plain, but carves and shaves regular geometric patterns into the pile like an obsessive topiarist. He orders double and treble rows of stitching to quilt fur and sheepskin into puffy diamonds. He will use leather and metal mesh as though they were woven fabrics, and demand as much from them, experimenting endlessly to find ways of making them more supple.' The textile-mill owners of Northern Italy half dreaded the visits of this most demanding taskmaster. As the magazine confirmed, 'He decides that he wants *this* effect for a fabric, he describes how it was done in the past or is still done in some distant land, and the mill-owner must struggle and experiment until he matches Versace's imagination.'

The mesh was Versace's own invention. In 1982, in collaboration with a German textile factory, Versace created Oroton, a fabric composed of tiny linked discs that behaved like liquid, pouring over the body and clinging to curves with dramatic, ductile grace. Its movement echoed the loose folds of a classical statue while its metallic texture gave it an effect that was utterly contemporary. As evidence of the range of Versace's imagination, and the way he gleaned influence from unlikely sources, the designer told *Vogue* that it was inspired by metal gauntlets used by farmers handling slaughtering knives. 'They were very beautiful objects, these gloves, like pieces of sculpture,' he said. 'I thought how interesting it would be to do something using this material. After all, Joan of Arc had her chain-mail.'

Overleaf *Versace's silver sarong and leather jacket. It was a most modern embodiment of eveningwear and very Versace: a couture gown worn with a punkish, street-tough leather jacket. Photograph by Herb Ritts.*

Before long, Oroton was in *Vogue*, depicted in such glittering items as 'the side-swept pewter dazzle dress', and a diamanté-studded cocktail gown, long in the front, short in the back, a garment of 'swathed, subtle gunmetal mail'. As expressive of his vision for his label as the Medusa logo, Oroton immediately assumed the status of house code. From its debut in 1982, the fabric featured in every Versace collection until the designer's death.

Nor did his technical experiments end there. While on a flight, Versace noticed that the material used to upholster airline seats was constructed without stitching, and was inspired to investigate whether it was possible to bond the seams of leather garments with a laser beam. (It was.) Such technical innovations tempered Versace's interest in historical modes of dressing, including, *Vogue* informed, 'rifling damask secrets from the Renaissance and jacquard expertise from the weavers of Lyons'. The clash of the contemporary and classic in his designs produced vividly original garments, and led to his work being celebrated in a 1985 display at the V&A, a significant honour for a brand only eight years old.

'The unmistakable bloom of luxury which rests on every Versace garment comes from the way he uses fabrics,' wrote Vogue. *A full-skirted evening gown is given further volume with quilted stitching in a floral pattern. Photograph by Michel Arnaud.*

Previous pages *In 1982, Versace created Oroton, photographed here by Albert Watson for its first appearance in* Vogue. *A fabric composed of tiny linked discs, it behaved like liquid, pouring over the body and clinging to curves with dramatic, ductile grace.*

Versace had by then established his ateliers on the top floor of a building on Via della Spiga, where teams of young designers translated his sketches. Versace wrote of his creative process: 'It begins with the written passage, imagining a scene from a novel, a woman who passes by dressed in black or a man with an intellectual air. Such scenes have always served me to envision the fashion that I want to design.' In reality it was a rather more practical and stressful undertaking. As he revealed to *Vogue*, 'The same afternoon after the show, I start on the next. I need one month to organise my plans, one month searching, studying fabrics, one month cutting and working in the factory. In the meantime, I go on with the drawings; then two months fittings.' He made hundreds of sketches, the best ones being worked into designs that were then translated into samples at the textile factories by Versace's skilful pattern cutters, or *modellisti*. The designer carried a notebook in which he jotted down his ideas. His former assistant informed Deborah Ball, 'Anything might be a source of inspiration – a flower bed, an architectural shape, the engraving on a piece of furniture, the floor of a church.' Ball described how Versace 'sketched in the evenings, on weekends, and during vacations, rising before dawn to visit the factories to check on samples or to meet with textile suppliers to go over new fabrics.' He was still

contracted to Callaghan and Genny – a profitable sideline that added exponentially to his workload. 'Whenever he was traveling, whether for vacation or for work, he sent dozens of faxes with sketches to his team, and called obsessively to see that they had followed his orders,' Ball wrote. 'He was so distracted that he stopped driving entirely, "for the safety of pedestrians," as he often joked.'

The hard work paid off. By the mid-eighties, Versace was living and operating in high style. *Vogue* described the lavish interiors of his atelier at Via della Spiga, a place of 'white marble neo-classic statues by Italian sculptors, Trotta and Paolini, plus beautiful Greek originals, glass and chrome tables, lamps by Zanuso for Artemide, black leather sofas and armchairs, floors and shelves in stone, the ceiling in natural wood with skylights, white freesias in a granite vase on his desk. In the huge open space studio – which will also be used for fashion shows – a French packaging designer, his American art director and two assistants are working on the bottle for Versace perfume by Charles of the Ritz. The choice is between a neo-classical sculpted bottle or a "natural" crystal. "Which one is more me?" wonders Gianni Versace.'

Versace's own apartments were located in the imposing, 45,000-square-foot/4180-square-metre, three-story palazzo on Via Gesù that he purchased in 1981 – horrifying the grandees of Milanese society. As they saw it, Gianni, Donatella and Santo were new money *arrivistes* from the rough, uncultured South, a place and a people and a déclassé style of dressing that was the very opposite of patrician Milan. (Their fears were to be later recognised as the palazzo became ground zero for Versace's exuberant fashion shows and celebrity fetes.)

A former convent, and once the family home of the Rizzoli publishing dynasty, Versace outfitted the palazzo with all the trimmings and panache, the classical statuary, leopard rugs, polished oak panelling, ornate plasterwork, baroque paintings, quattrocento antiques, gold, gilt and marble of a Medici prince. Aptly, Versace's four-poster bed was formerly the property of a fourteenth-century Medici. To a newspaper he once revealed the daily habit it inspired: '"I look at the little angel first in the morning," Versace murmurs, pointing to the figures painted on the interior of the wooden canopy of his bed.

"I pray, 'Please help me another day.'"' By 1986, the palazzo, with its pretty courtyards and secret roof garden, also housed his ateliers and offices. *Vogue* recorded in 1988, 'With the growing prosperity of Italy itself, Milan's designers have created for themselves what looks like an unassailable corporate splendour reminiscent of nothing so much as the courts of the High Renaissance.' Andy Warhol revealed in a diary entry: 'Thursday Jan 22 1987: Lunch with Gianni Versace, went to his Milan castle. Rizzoli's old castle. Big Roman and Greek statues that Suzie Frankfurt got Versace to buy. It was grand, huge, so glamorous.'

Overleaf Dramatic, sensuous leather dominated Vogue's coverage of the designer in the eighties (left). Photograph by Terence Donovan. Janice Dickinson in 1979 (right) photographed by Alex Chatelain, coquettish in ochre, khaki, violet and pink print chiffon, an early experiment in pattern and colour for Genny.

Versace was able to afford such luxury, and to cultivate increasingly extravagant spending habits, because of the astute business arrangements established by his brother. Santo had reinvested the millions Gianni was making from contract work into factories and advertising. He negotiated licences for outside companies to create ancillary products, such as shoes, fragrance, sunglasses, jewellery, watches and bags, and opened stores in prestigious shopping sites, including Paris and Rome, and franchised boutiques in locations as distant as Singapore. In 1985 the house launched Istante, a diffusion line designed by Versace's boyfriend, Antonio D'Amico, that offered a conservative take on Versace style. By 1986 the company was making sales of $220 million.

After the death of Gianni's mother, Franca Versace, in 1978, Donatella had quit her university studies and come to live with Gianni in Milan. As the success of the house grew, she became a key member of his team. Donatella's contribution was to bring a contemporary edge – and a pulsing sexuality – to the Versace look. 'She is the modern woman', Versace declared, 'she pushes me to be more free and to make my clothes more feminine.' As *Vogue* related: 'When Donatella said shorter, Gianni got out the shears.' 'My mother was the strong one, and when my mother die, I took her place,' Donatella told *New York* magazine. 'I thought of myself as the one who really was able to tell Gianni the truth, because with a big designer, nobody is able. That's the big threat for a big designer.'

ROCKSTAR
AQVA
STORIA
LA CVCINA
ITALIANA
ARCHEO
FIERA

With Santo as company director, and Donatella as muse and sounding board, the house of Versace was from its inception, and in the Italian tradition, a family business. Of the benefits of working with his siblings, Versace said: 'We can fight at 6 o'clock and have a nice dinner at 8.'

Meanwhile, the designer's prestige grew. His daywear designs included large, loose-cut, shoulder-padded jackets and neat black skirt suits that echoed the easy aesthetic and fashion dominance of designers such as Ralph Lauren, Calvin Klein and Versace's arch-rival, Armani. The latter's new take on suiting, as showcased to devastating effect on Richard Gere and Lauren Hutton in the 1980 movie, *American Gigolo*, had become the uniform of chic women everywhere in the eighties. Armani's designs, in their muted, minimal tastefulness, were a total contradiction of Versace style. *The New Yorker* defined the dichotomy, saying, 'If other designers' clothes tell the world you're fun in bed, Armani's clothes tell the world [...] you know how to live.' As American *Vogue* editor Anna Wintour commented, 'Versace was always sort of the "mistress" to Armani's "wife."'

The New Woman: Linda Evangelista wears a navy wool polka-dot jacket and silk flared skirt. Eighties' working women needed an executive wardrobe, clothes with an assertive silhouette to match the new mood. Photograph by Eddy Kohli.

Overleaf *The house couture line, Atelier Versace, launched in 1989. The sharp silhouette of a 1990 navy suit, worn to smouldering effect by Tatjana Patitz and photographed by Patrick Demarchelier, is praised by* Vogue *for its 'unimpeachable cut'.*

Throughout their careers, the pair exchanged frequent, veiled (and not so veiled) barbs. As Gianni told *The New Yorker* in 1997, 'There is a little bit of "nasty" on both sides, because, you know, business is business. For twenty years, he's had to look at me, and I've always had to – well, there have always been the two of us in Milan.' He continued, 'For him it was jealousy, jealousy, jealousy. We are totally different.' He was equally blunt about Armani's style of design: 'I dress a woman who is more beautiful, more glamorous. I love women. He, on the other hand, has a type of woman who is always a little sombre, a little dull.'

Whatever their differences, the success of both designers spoke to a cultural movement shaping the late eighties. The politics of private enterprise in Europe and America created demand for a new aesthetic. Women, encouraged to enter the workplace, needed an executive wardrobe, clothes with an assertive silhouette to match the new mood.

‘I DRESS
A WOMAN
WHO IS MORE
BEAUTIFUL,
MORE
GLAMOROUS.’

GIANNI VERSACE

The power suit was a shoulder-padded jacket and short, tight skirt, as praised in *Vogue* by Janet Street-Porter for its dual ability to 'get us a job and get us sex'. The young, upwardly mobile professional – or yuppie – had money to spend and wanted to be seen spending it on designer brands. Versace's clothes – an open celebration of money, power and sex – were emblematic of the age. (Sean Penn wore Versace to marry Madonna, while Bruce Springsteen sported the label on tour.) Meanwhile, the widespread use of Lycra seemed expressly made for the designer's lithe, sinuous, unapologetically sexy garments. An expensively toned body – the highest indicator of eighties' success – was to be flaunted, preferably in Versace.

Yasmin Le Bon in Versace's barely there, beaded black lace camisole. Photograph by Hans Feurer.

Previous pages *'A black velvet dress is my earliest memory,' wrote Versace. An eighties' rendering of the nostalgic design is lent womanly attitude with the addition of sheer black stockings and leather gloves (left). Photograph by Albert Watson. 'The power suit, à la Versace (right). A young Naomi Campbell, photographed by Eddy Kohli, wears the designer's exuberant, colour-blocking, shoulder-padded silhouette.*

Vogue captured the moment, reporting in 1987, 'At all the new collections short appears in every guise, with fashion victim implicit for all but the youngest and leggiest in the jailbait extreme.' It continued, 'Shock is no longer the question, it is a matter of balance and beauty, with bosoms alarmingly visible at times.' With safe sex and AIDS on the news agenda, the magazine commented, 'Now that bodies are just for looking at, 3D flesh is key.' In its pages, a new variety of glamazon model articulated the shorter-tighter aesthetic proposed by Versace, Azzedine Alaïa and Thierry Mugler: Yasmin Le Bon modelled Versace's lace camisole, a daring concoction that revealed glimpses of naked flesh, while Naomi Campbell sported a colour-blocked miniskirt suit. 'I like sexy clothes,' said Versace. 'They express joy. They break barriers.' This age of bold-faced glamour and monied excess found a face in 'The small skirt big hair brigade,' wrote *Vogue*, citing its members: 'Marla Maples, Jerry Hall, Mandy Smith, Joan Collins.' The latter, *Dynasty's* Alexis Carrington, who vamped on screen in furs and diamonds, was interviewed by *Vogue* in 1988 and photographed, naturally, in Versace

By 1988, Versace had assembled his elements of style. As *Vogue* was moved to report: 'Italian design may be said to have moved out of its early Renaissance period into a phase of full-blown baroque.

The Italian appetite for *more* has recently shown itself in the theatrical presentation of the shortest and tightest of skirts, the widest of shoulders, the highest of hairstyles and heels. Foremost in the new Italian baroque is undoubtedly Gianni Versace, as he surpasses himself in each subsequent show with yet more breathtaking inventions – the trouser-skirt with half a sarong on one side, half a pair of leggings on the other, or panniered dresses gathered into harem pants at the ankle.' Versace matched leopard print with baroque patterns, beaded leggings under layers of duchess silk skirts that echoed the eighteenth-century dresses of a Fragonard painting. The contrasts felt fresh and innovative. In 1989 *Vogue* showed a jacket embroidered with circus motifs, with a trapeze artist swinging, upside down, on the model's shoulder. Combining technique, handcraft skills, fun, colour and expert cut, it was typical Versace. *The New York Times* reported of a 1989 Versace show: 'Three times the audience members stood and applauded because they felt the peak of design had been reached. Each time there was more.'

Characteristic Versace: an exquisite, circus-themed, exuberantly embroidered jacket photographed by Patrick Demarchelier.

Previous pages *Lycra could have been expressly made for the designer's sinuous, slinky garments. A stretch gloss Lycra tube dress (left) photographed by Patrick Demarchelier, wraps a supermodel body. Versace expressed the eighties' concept of empowered femininity with a forthright and expensively dressed sensuality (right). Photograph by Neil Kirk.*

Capitalising on his celebrity and his company's achievements, in January 1989 Versace debuted a couture line, Atelier Versace, with an informal presentation at the Musée d'Orsay in Paris. The city's grey and *soigné* couture houses were suspicious of Versace, a ready-to-wear designer – from Italy, no less – muscling in on the sacred territory of such fabled names as Dior and Chanel. Equally, there were those within Versace's house who questioned why its namesake would bother with the exorbitant expense and potential disaster involved in entering the refined world of haute couture. Even French houses understood couture was a loss-leader, albeit a magnificent showcase for a designer's ideas. As *The New York Times* attested, 'Only love of his craft could make a designer undertake such a risk as couture, when he had no need of the publicity and the risk might never yield rewards.'

But bold gestures were a Versace trademark. In January 1990 the designer staged his first runway presentation for Atelier Versace.

With inimitable showmanship, it was held at the Paris Ritz, with a catwalk built over the hotel's swimming pool – 'at a cost of £20,000 and the considerable irritation of some guests, although the latter were promised that all would be back to normal by the following morning,' *Vogue* reported. Paraded before an audience filled with Hollywood stars, the rigorously well-made collection – garments built from the inside out, with an 'inner architecture', according to Joan Juliet Buck – featured sequined bodysuits worn with frock coats, encrusted bustiers teamed with slim-fit trousers, and a bias-cut silk dress embellished with over-sized chains that slithered down the model's spine. This was the apex of Versace style, combining exquisite tailoring, colour, print and surface detail in looks that celebrated the female form, and seemed to celebrate life too. Beaded minidresses, cheekily embroidered with the Eiffel Tower or the words 'Au Revoir Paris', mixed pop culture and couture, broadening the appeal and reach of this supremely French hand-craft industry that was (then as now) reported to be in its dying gasps.

It was a collection that was identifiably Versace: modelled by glamorous women, worn to thrill, a concentration of his ideas that included, as *Women's Wear Daily* reported, 'more feathers, pearls, rhinestones, jewels, tassels, beading and embroidery than Paris has seen in some time'. After the 45-minute show the audience broke into cheering and applause. Versace had conquered the eighties and, with one extraordinary show, looked set to extend his influence into the next decade. 'I want to be a designer for my time,' he said. It was a sign of things to come.

Versace, said Vogue, was 'foremost in the new Italian baroque', as seen in this example of off-the-shoulder glamour for Joan Collins, photographed by Snowdon.

Previous pages *Helena Christensen models a zodiac-inspired minidress (left) and a bead-embellished bodice (right). Photographs by Sante D'Orazio.*

Overleaf *Versace's understated luxury for daywear (left): a suede jacket with oriental gold embroidery teamed with green suede jodhpurs. Photograph by Neil Kirk. Cindy Crawford showcases Versace's dazzling couture showstopper (right) – a tailored cashmere jacket and encrusted bodysuit – on the streets of Paris. Photograph by Arthur Elgort.*

> 'I like sexy clothes. They express joy. They break barriers.'
>
> GIANNI VERSACE

‘FASHION IS NOT JUST A PIECE OF FABRIC. NO, NO, NO. IT’S AN ATTITUDE, IT’S A WAY TO EXPRESS. IT’S YOU.’

GIANNI VERSACE

VOGUE
DEC
£2·50
ROYAL PORTRAITS: THE PRINCESS OF WALES
MODERN
MADONNAS ... WARHOL'S ANIMAL CRACKERS
SNOWDON'S RARE BREEDS

By the end of the eighties, an entirely new breed of model had begun to appear in the pages of *Vogue*. In 1988, the magazine photographed Christy Turlington and Linda Evangelista, praising their 'strong personalities blessed with the ability and the genes to project the passing dreams and aspirations of current fashion. At peak desirability, their looks command escalating fortunes.' Together with Naomi Campbell, the models became a triumvirate so ubiquitous on billboards and magazine spreads that they were known as 'the Trinity'. These models did not conform to stereotype. 'Each girl is an individual, an identifiable character on the page,' *Vogue* reported. Their only shared aspect was a womanly aesthetic, 'busts and hips that go in and out, the way women are meant to. There's nothing cutesy or vulnerable about them – they are sexy, sexual – though some men might feel intimidated by the grand scale of it all.'

In a piece of winning and utterly shameless direct marketing, Versace embellishes a sleek catsuit with beaded Vogue covers – for a Vogue cover. Photograph by Patrick Demarchelier.

To mark the new decade, *Vogue* commissioned Peter Lindbergh to photograph Tatjana Patitz, Evangelista, Turlington, Campbell and Cindy Crawford for an iconic January 1990 cover. On seeing it, George Michael promptly cast the quintet in his music video for 'Freedom! '90', in which the models, barely dressed, lip-synced to the track. From being confined to magazines and fashion spreads, these models were suddenly recognisable personalities: the supermodel era was born.

Versace was quick to recognise the commercial potential in using this handful of girls to sell his fashions. Editorial models and runway models were traditionally distinct categories: runway girls had the dimensions for catwalk samples and a graceful walk, but not the singular beauty required for fashion images. Versace had already brought fizz to his catwalks by importing the high-profile faces who starred in his campaigns. But never to such magnificent effect as in March 1991, when the designer showed his autumn/winter collection on the highest-paid, most sought-after models, including Claudia Schiffer, Stephanie Seymour, Carla Bruni, Helena Christensen and Karen Mulder, wearing thigh-high PVC 'hooker' boots, baby-doll dresses, leather jackets and embroidered velvet bustiers that borrowed their silhouette from a previous century.

'HIS SHORT IS SHORTEST, HIS BRIGHT IS BRIGHTEST, HIS SEXY BLATANT.'

VOGUE

Linda, Cindy, Naomi and Christy lip-syncing to George Michael's 'Freedom! '90' in the finale of Versace's March 1991 show. 'He was the first to realize the value of the supermodel,' said Anna Wintour.

Overleaf *Versace joyfully plundered low culture for inspiration. Leather-bar dress codes mix with Greek antiquity in a key-patterned studded black leather jacket and pleated skirt (left). Photograph by Sante D'Orazio.*
A well-cut shorts suit (right) undergoes the Versace effect by way of a gilt Medusa-head belt, gilt buttons and gilt-chain slingbacks. Photograph by Terence Donovan.

For a finale, the quartet of Cindy, Linda, Naomi and Christy, a vision of big hair and prowling sexuality – their appearance at a reported cost of $100,000 – bobbed arm-in-arm down the catwalk in swinging mini-dresses miming the lyrics to 'Freedom! '90'. It was an historic fashion moment, simultaneously anointing these women as the definition of nineties glamazon beauty, and Versace as the designer of the new decade.

As Donatella later told *Vogue*, 'It was my brother who created the phenomenon of the supermodel. He made the models into celebrities, as he understood that the more famous they became, the better it would be for him.' As if spurred by the sheer scale of supermodel glamour, Versace's ideas reached full expression in the early nineties. His collection for spring/summer 1992 was an explosion of heraldic pattern, oceanic motifs, beading, leopard print, embellishment, gilt, embroidery, chains, Medusa logos, gold, black, skintight leggings, jewelled cropped jackets, printed silk shirts, body suits and a definitive Versace print: rococo vines mixed with leopard spots, a concoction he dubbed 'Wild Baroque'. With inspired bravado, Versace matched denim shirts with Duchess-worthy layered lace skirts, while a delicately beaded silk evening dress featured the faces of Marilyn Monroe and James Dean in a Warhol-inspired print. *The New York Times* wrote of the collection's 'gorgeous excess', praising its modernity. 'Where other designers were tentative, he was forceful. He displayed a complete understanding of what makes fashion work, both the rational and the irrational elements. And so this collection will have a powerful influence.' As Versace confessed in *Signatures*, 'Excess is entertaining, eccentricity stimulating. Only one rule applies, spontaneity.'

Flounced silk, animal print layers fall into a long train over a short moiré skirt, worn on a vampish Naomi Campbell. Photograph by Tyen.

Overleaf *Karen Mulder wearing Versace's signature print, a clashing compound of rococo vines mixed with leopard spots that he dubbed 'Wild Baroque' (left). Printed seashells scattered on a white denim jacket with matching jeans and starfish belt set with pastel rhinestones (right). Photograph by Sante D'Orazio.*

Those who subscribed to the minimal, cerebral look of the Japanese designers of the eighties were appalled by Versace's maximalist vision for the new decade. Critics were also divided when, for autumn/winter 1992, Versace presented a collection that featured, amongst beautifully sculptural jackets and studded leather skirts, the world's most famous models trussed up in bondage-inspired straps, buckles and harnesses.

The designer – who borrowed widely for his work, variously inspired by Warhol, Ancient Egypt, Classical Greece – was here animated by the iconography of the gay nightclub scene, describing the collection as 'a fun bit of sado-masochism.' Holly Brubach of *The New Yorker* took a darker view: 'There were people who loved it, who thought it was brilliant, the greatest thing he had ever done. And others of us, mostly women, could barely evaluate the design aspect of it because we were so offended.'

A long crêpe dress with satin strapped bodice from Versace's critic-dividing bondage collection in 1992. Photograph by Tyen.

Overleaf *'They said these clothes belonged only in a leather bar,' said Versace of the criticism of his bondage collection, but, as Vogue wrote: 'Leather will go to the ball, with ribboned bodices and gilt accents. The voluminous skirts are split high, just for kicks.' Photograph by Arthur Elgort.*

Not for the first time, a charge of vulgarity was levelled at Versace. He viewed the epithet, and the news headlines it garnered, as a kneejerk reaction in the face of innovation, a sign of timidity (not an emotion much in use *chez* Versace) expressed by those who lacked imagination and a sense of fun. He told an Italian TV channel, 'Vulgarity is for people who are frightened, not for us.' Indeed, in retrospect and as photographed in *Vogue*, Versace's bondage dresses are notable not for their power to shock but for their beautiful construction, for bodices created from a complicated web of strategically placed straps. On the model Tyra Banks, leather skirts, soft as silk, were cut from voluptuous quantities of material and draped and gathered in a style that – leather, studs and thigh-splits notwithstanding – would not have looked amiss at the court of Versailles.

If such a look now feels familiar, its shock safely defused, it's a testament to how emphatically Versace established an overt sexuality in the fashion vocabulary. A critic might not like it, they would have grounds to call it tasteless, too bright, too brash, too short, too tight, too much of everything, but it was never truly vulgar – *near* nudity was encouraged, but Versace's dresses were exquisite creations, and even when breasts were wrapped only in leather straps there was a strict architecture at work. His aim was not to embarrass women but to celebrate them. As Hamish Bowles commented, with their 'preoccupations with luxurious display and sensual gratification', Versace's clothes displayed a 'delicious rejection of mimsy good taste'.

‘VULGARITY IS FOR PEOPLE WHO ARE FRIGHTENED, NOT FOR US.’

GIANNI VERSACE

Here were clothes to have fun in, to seduce; life could not possibly be boring while wearing a Versace dress. In an interview with the designer, *Vogue* attested: 'When he does something, he does it *con brio*; his short is shortest, his bright is brightest, his sexy blatant: "I like one thing or the other. In the middle there is something that doesn't work."' And, of course, scandal was good for business. As a smiling Versace told *Vanity Fair*, 'They said these clothes belonged only in a leather bar. And now, last night, there were 200 socialites in bondage.'

Put simply, if you wanted to dress like a supermodel in the early nineties – and who didn't? – it meant dressing in Versace. It was newly possible too, with the introduction of diffusion lines offering Versace style to the masses. In 1991, the company launched Signature, a secondary collection with watered-down versions of Versace classics that were more accessible in price. In the same year the house presented Versatile, a range for fuller-figured women (that nevertheless included leopard catsuits), and Versace Jeans Couture, a casual line selling $200 jeans, capitalizing on the popularity of designer denim. In 1993 a range of homewares was launched, for which Versace signatures – baroque patterns, leopard print, Greek motifs – were transposed onto plates, bed linen and teapots and advertised, in high Versace style, by Claudia Schiffer and Sylvester Stallone, naked but for two extremely well-placed plates. Opulent stores around the world sold the Versace dream; on Bond Street, a former bank was turned into a Versace boutique at a cost of $6 million. The designer's empire spanned the globe, a byword for Italian luxury, for supermodels and rock stars – a heady association that powered the sales of ancillary items, even down to a pair of Versace brand tights.

It was almost irrelevant whether or not you liked his designs since they could neither be ignored nor avoided. Versace's success spoke for a new moment in fashion: the designer era. Label consciousness in the eighties had changed the clothing industry. In the nineties, fashion was no longer the niche preserve of the knowledgeable few. Newspapers now used full-colour images of the supermodels to sell copies. Ready-to-wear was growing more profitable year by year with more designers joining the schedule to show in Paris, New York, London and Milan.

Versace paid handsomely to secure the likes of Karen Mulder, Linda Evangelista and Carla Bruni to walk on his catwalk and appear in his advertising campaigns. The strategy worked: the Versace house was forever fused with the amplified glamour of the supermodel moment.

The biggest designers – the likes of Calvin Klein and Armani – had become high-profile individuals in their own right, interviewed in magazines and on television. In Italy, Versace was a celebrity equal to those lining his front rows, a Medici prince of the fashion scene, featuring regularly in gossip pages.

The lavish way in which the house of Versace conducted its business – where sales and image were burnished by an expensive cocktail of advertising, catwalk shows, exclusive model contracts, entertaining and celebrity relationships – became fashion's new mode. As *Vogue* reported from Milan in 1990: 'A five day agenda might include Krizia's intimate dinner for 500; half a dozen buffets, a cosy supper at a Ferragamo *palazzo*, and a midnight expedition to the suburbs to see Gianni Versace, Jane Fonda and 1,500 other guests mix business with pleasure.' This policy of entertaining journalists at home, the magazine continued, of 'flying in stars to raise the glamour quotient of their shows, doesn't make Milanese designers more frivolous than their counterparts elsewhere. It is simply the way they like to do business. All night partying, in their terms, means all night selling.' And nothing beat a Versace party, not with Donatella leading the charge.

Previous pages *Versace's take on the new spirit of grunge: a stripped back – but still seductive – metallic PVC mini. Photograph by Mikael Jansson. Anti-glamour photographers reflected the new mood. Corinne Day captured a made-under Linda Evangelista in Versace's poppy-red silk tube.*

Gianni's daring designs of the early nineties, his eager use of supermodels and top photographers to communicate his designs, his careful patronage of a celebrity fan base, were in no small part due to his sister's encouragement. Slight, with a mane of blonde hair, outfitted in high heels and tight clothes, Donatella was 'the epitome of the kind of glamour her brother idealises every season on the catwalk,' *Vogue* informed. 'Luckily for the Versaces it is an image of desirability

'Excess is entertaining, eccentricity stimulating. Only one rule applies, spontaneity.'

GIANNI VERSACE

that is recognised everywhere, from the King's Road to Rodeo Drive, and it is selling like crazy.' Donatella said of her influence, 'We are two strong personalities. Santo has a good equilibrium, and balances us. But every season I say to Gianni, don't be too safe! Take risks! You cannot please everybody.' In recognition of her contribution, in 1993 Gianni put her in charge of designing collections for Versus, the house's younger, contemporary label.

Family *was* business at Versace. *Vogue* described a visit to the house in 1990: 'We have already been to the Versace offices in the Via della Spiga, Milan's most prestigious shopping strip, where an unsmiling, dark-suited Santo Versace, Gianni's older brother and president of finance of the Gruppo Versace, is on his way to a meeting; already visited more offices in the Via Sant' Andrea, where Gianni's adored younger sister Donatella, vice-president, is at work; and have been to yet another office that stores sample collections, in the street bumping into a puffed-out Paul Beck' – Donatella's Versace model husband whom she married in 1983 – 'as he rushes between one base of the Versace empire and the other.' At the Versace palazzo on the Via Gesù, 'One wing is devoted to design and to production of the new Atelier couture collection, including a large, cool, private room of mirrored wardrobes in which VIPs can be shown and fitted for the heavily beaded dresses they so often buy. Upstairs are housed the twenty-four seamstresses who tenderly hand-finish all that beading, and Versace's team of eight young Italian, Chinese and Japanese design assistants, all dressed in black, working happily in shiny black, modern offices with coloured pencils and brilliant fragments of Versace's clashing prints arranged neatly on their desks.'

In 1990 Linda Evangelista gave a quote to a magazine that seemed to encapsulate the best and worst of the supermodel phenomenon: 'We have this expression, Christy and I. We don't wake up for less than ten thousand dollars a day.' Nor did they have to. Didier Fernandez, director at DNA Models, told *Vogue*: 'I'd have Valentino on one phone, Versace on the other, and it was like an auction to see who would get the girl.' Cindy Crawford said, 'All of a sudden we were able to say,

"Well, we're only flying Concorde" or "We're staying at the Ritz." And if they wanted us they had to do it. And I think that the powers that be in the fashion industry might not have liked the fact that a 20-year-old girl had that much power.'

The backlash began in the following year. A fresh feeling in fashion proposed by Marc Jacobs's flannel shirts and beanie hats for Perry Ellis, and by a new manifestation of flat-chested beauty expressed by models Kate Moss, Stella Tennant and Shalom Harlow, was captured in naturalistic photographs by David Sims, Mario Sorrenti and Corinne Day. *Vogue* wrote: 'Japanese film crews have jammed the flight paths to Heathrow, eager to ask Kate Moss, a waif from Croydon with limp hair, wide eyes and a million-dollar contract with Calvin Klein, the questions they put to Linda Evangelista two years ago.' In its deliberate anti-glamour, grunge – as the style and movement became known – was the antithesis of the Versace look. (A *Vogue* headline decried: 'Boobs – where are they now?') Nevertheless, Donatella was quick to encourage Gianni to co-opt Kate Moss and, later, Stella Tennant into Versace's catwalk shows and campaigns. The magazine reported: 'Gianni Versace has succumbed to the revised aesthetic.' However, he was not immediately sold on Tennant's androgynous appeal, as the model later informed *Vogue*: 'I was on the catwalk mid-rehearsal – Gianni stopped the music and said, "*Who* is that?" They cancelled me immediately.'

A white catsuit with exaggeratedly flared legs expresses Versace's experiment in bohemian seventies resort glamour. Photograph by Mario Testino.

Overleaf *'Loveliness, fragility and a subliminal take on grunge,' said* Vogue *of Versace's embroidered and beaded tulle sheath dresses and skirt worn over striped Lycra bodies. Photograph by Andrew Macpherson.*

The nineties' shift from sharp tailoring to softness, from maximalist fashion to stripped-back beauty, were converted into a moderated glamour in Versace's work. He offered a style of jet-set hippie luxe characterised in *Vogue* in an unembellished – but form-fitting – white jumpsuit with flaring bell-bottoms, photographed on Christy Turlington by Mario Testino. Versace's take on grunge was mostly subliminal. Outfitted in his 1993 couture collection for *Vogue*, the slouching poses of models of the moment Emma Balfour and Rosemary Ferguson did little to contradict the essential, lively glossiness of Versace's beaded tulle sheaths and rhinestone sandals.

‘COUTURE SHOULD BE SPECIAL BUT ALSO ACCESSIBLE.’

GIANNI VERSACE

While 'heroin chic' predominated, the house of Versace was a haven of reassuring luxury and womanly femininity. In an article from 1993, *Vogue* followed eighteen-year-old student Jemima Goldsmith as she shopped for her first Versace couture gown; the magazine described a collection of 'swaggering plush velvet trouser suits in raspberry and purple, tiny slips made of exquisite Chantilly lace, about as substantial as the froth on a cappuccino; a midnight-blue cashmere coat with sun-ray pleats that bounce just above the knees,' looks that were 'as shimmering and carefree as a swarm of butterflies' and just about as far as you could get from grunge chic. Commenting on couture's dusty laws and precepts, Versace offered an irreverent riposte that verged on sacrilege, revealing a democratic – commercially minded – view of fashion: 'I hate rules. What is this mania for doing everything by hand? Stupid and pretentious, that's what. Machines can do some things better than hand. Couture should be special but also accessible.' *Vogue* revealed he was even selling versions of his favourite Atelier Versace outfits in his boutiques, offering haute couture for less.

Vogue writes, 'Pretty woman and her couturier: three fittings and six weeks after she first saw it on the runway, Jemima Goldsmith and Gianni Versace enjoy the £6000 final product – a curvy black wool crepe pinafore and silk satin and lace shirt with knife-point collar.' Photograph by Tiziano Magni.

Overleaf *Versace's acid-green minidress modelled by the tall, glamorous figure of Nadja Auermann, and photographed for Vogue's 1994 catwalk guide by Nick Knight.*

By 1994, fashion had grown tired of the waif look. The international catwalks offered a much-desired return to glamour, epitomised in the rise of the Teutonic, blonde and unfeasibly long-legged model, Nadja Auermann. *Vogue* reported: 'If Kate Moss's timing made her the cipher for one kind of fashion, Nadja is helping to usher in another. There is a confident, sexy edginess defining fashion now that is light years away from the dreamy, lyrical mood of last year.' Versace, of course, was already there. In the mid-nineties, his house codes – colour, fabric, cut and contrast – had become sleeker, with fewer embellishments and a sophisticated sexuality that echoed fashion's new seriousness, while remaining highly alluring to red-carpet customers such as Madonna and Demi Moore.

For spring/summer 1994, he tempered day looks of girlish mini-kilts and lace shirts with evening gowns of sari-like, body-conscious draping.

‘THE WORLD OF GIANNI VERSACE GIVES AN OPTIMISM TO THE HUMAN SPIRIT.’

ANDRÉ LEON TALLEY

®
VOGUE
catwalk
guide
in association with
Lancôme
All the news from
London, Paris,
Milan, New York

There were also long, lean black column dresses, slashed at the chest, waist, hip and thigh and held perilously together with Medusa-embossed gold safety pins, a feat of engineering, corsetry, and hope. This was Versace at his utmost, infusing a fashion classic – the little black dress – with a punk edge and palpable sexuality. On the catwalk the look was spectacular. On the red carpet it was world news. When the voluptuous and then-unknown Elizabeth Hurley wore a Versace safety-pin gown to attend her boyfriend Hugh Grant's film premier, it made her a star. The dress became That Dress. Yet, as Hurley admitted to *Vogue*, before she had tried on the dress in the press office loo, 'I had hardly heard of Versace.' Hurley later revealed, 'I didn't feel remotely self-conscious in it because it was exquisitely cut and didn't shift a millimetre all night.'

On a wave of thirties' and forties' fashions, corsets and lingerie dressing as proposed by the likes of John Galliano and Tom Ford at Gucci, by January 1995, *Vogue* reported: 'Bosoms, bottoms, waists and hips – the lot' were back in style. 'The nineties silhouette,' informed *Vogue*, 'has shaped up.' Nick Knight photographed Helena Christensen reclining across a motorbike in a pale blush chiffon Versace dress with matching exposed knickers. Here was 'The return of the good-time girl', the magazine announced, a freshly re-discovered species of woman who dressed short and tight and to be noticed. Versace's brand of overt glamour more than fitted the bill, as was evidenced by a Marc Hom shot of Carolyn Murphy, her skin pearled with sweat, her eye make-up smudged, wearing a pink chain-mail crop top and matching mini.

Worn by Liz Hurley to the premiere of Four Weddings and a Funeral, *Versace's iconic creation of silk, Lycra and oversized gold safety pins became one of the most famous dresses in the world.*

previous pages *Short and sweet: a pastel pink bouclé tweed Versace suit (left), photographed by Mario Testino, has a coquettish appeal. Kate Moss in a chequerboard skirt (right) by Versus, the diffusion line designed by Versace's sister, Donatella. Photograph by Wayne Maser.*

'These clothes are not for shrinking violets.'

VOGUE

‘I AM CREATING A FASHION THAT IS ALIVE. DRESSES THAT MOVE.’

GIANNI VERSACE

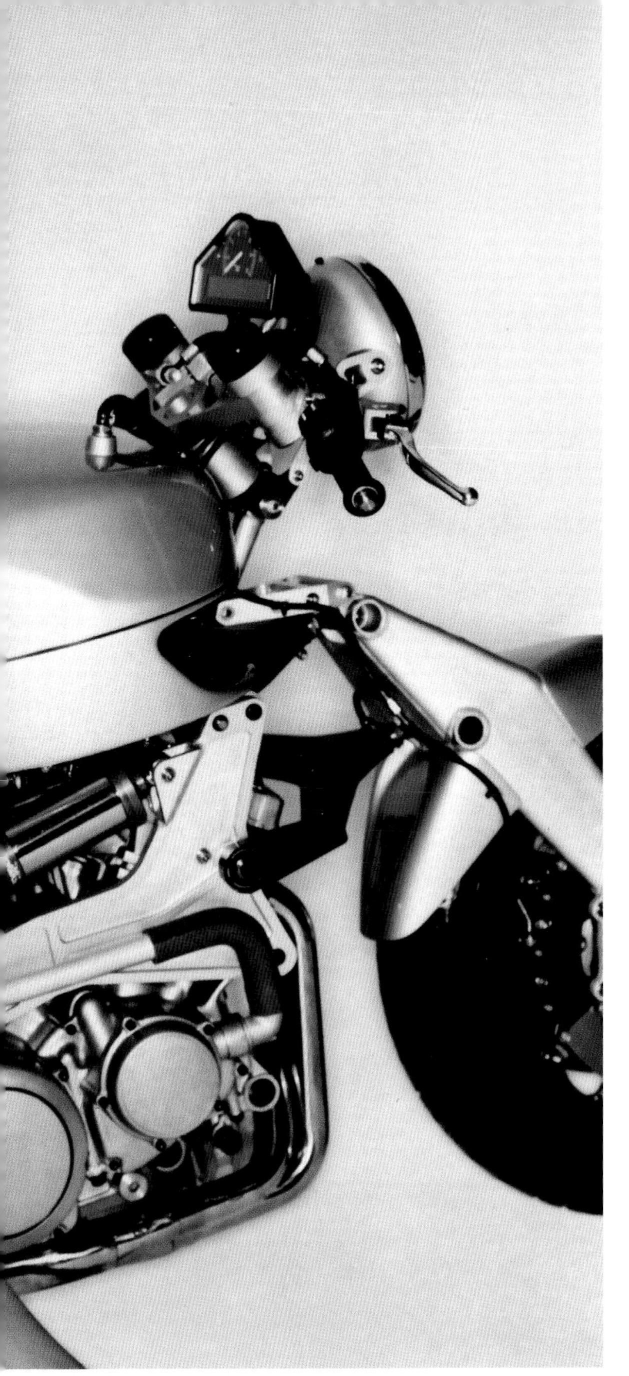

'A SUPREMELY SELF-ASSURED FEMININE SEXUALITY.'

VOGUE

As fashion went full-throttle for the fifties, Helena Christensen was draped by Nick Knight across the chrome body of a motorbike in Versace's sugar-pink layered chiffon dress with matching hot pants.

Previous pages *Stella Tennant, one of the new breed of androgynous beauties championed by Donatella Versace, lent edge to a tight leather jacket with sheepskin sleeves worn over a satin evening dress. Photograph by David Sims.*

By 1997, Versace was at the head of an estimated $1 billion empire. He imagined his customer as, 'a woman who listens to classical music but enjoys rock, who reads *The New Yorker* and Calvino but can have a laugh at gossipy chronicles, who adores wearing Versace with Calvin Klein jeans or Versace jeans with a Chanel jacket.' A statement that spoke of Versace's inclusiveness, the warmth of his personal view, his ability to straddle and find inspiration in both museums and nightclubs and a democratic notion of fashion as expressed by the ever-expanding diffusion lines that traded under his name.

'There's a return to colour which, when used with lightweight chain mail, produces a glittering new femininity,' Versace told Vogue *in 1997 – as Carolyn Murphy demonstrates in a pink and black rhinestone cropped top and miniskirt. Photograph by Marc Hom.*

Overleaf *'The best self defence for evening is a cutaway golden chain-mail dress,' said* Vogue. *Photographed against a grunge-worthy industrial backdrop, Linda Evangelista wears Versace's Oroton mini. Photograph by Glen Luchford.*

As Amy Spindler wrote in *The New York Times*, Versace had 'an understanding that his client is a woman of the world who knows what the hottest thing in the wind is, but loves him best. In that, he is not a man of a certain time; he is a man of the times, and his customer will never look old, tired or lost in a sea of change, because he is not.' His collections were full of fresh ideas, his silhouette had become sleek without losing interest or innovation. 'At first I had to do a bit of "scream" to have real success, but now I don't need to do those things,' he told *The New Yorker*. By 1997 his star was established. The name Versace had come to stand for an exaggerated vision of money, power, sex and success – an achievement of the designer's imagination, but also his singular work ethic. 'The world of Gianni Versace gives an optimism to the human spirit', wrote André Leon Talley. 'The world of fashion in the eighties and in the nineties owes much to the confident and bold Universe of Versace's sophisticated sensuality and sexuality, it is the imagined universe of fantasy and magic. And swaggering luxe.'

'There is nothing diffident about his work.
It has always been remarkable for its self-assurance
and adventurousness.'

VOGUE

THE LIFE VERSACE

By the time *Vogue* paid a call to Versace at his Milan palazzo in 1990, the house – and the designer himself – had cultivated a reputation for operatic excess expressed not only in his slinky fashions but in the Versace mode of being, in the decadence that defined the life Versace: that is, life with the volume turned up. This was not only a matter of character, since the designer was a warm and generous person who thought nothing of spending $2 million in one afternoon on furnishings for his sister's apartment, but also a form of image control. From the outset, Versace sought to create an identity and a sense of permanence for his label, using artworks and a portfolio of opulent properties, lavish parties, expensive advertising, aggrandising coffee-table books and the best of everything, from models to photographers, as a distracting sheen, to effect an impression of the house of Versace – though only a few years old – as a place of heritage and inviolable luxury.

Gianni and Donatella, photographed at Gianni's art- and antiquity-filled home, Villa Fontanelle, on Lake Como. His houses were an outlandish expression of luxury and the construction of a powerful fantasy. Madonna said of a visit there: 'I felt like a spoilt princess.'

Compensating for his humble background in Reggio di Calabria, in the fullness of his success the designer's tastes ran to high ostentation, to homes outfitted in a king's ransom of gilt and gold and marble. Though he might have wished it otherwise, the name Versace was not a byword for unmatched elegance, but the opposite: a symbol of a type of extravagance common amongst a shiny new breed of eighties' and nineties' millionaires, who shared a maximalist aesthetic that ran right up to the edge of vulgarity and often toppled straight in. Not that the designer cared for anyone else's judgment. (Why should he, when so many wanted to emulate his style?) In life as in his fashions, Versace felt no impulse to capitulate to dry and dreary, humourless good taste.

There was something celebratory in the sheer proportion and force of his spending habits and lifestyle. Residing in such grandeur was an act of will as much as discernment. The palazzo's residential wing, as described in *Vogue*, was symbolic of the Versace experience, being 'something akin to what the British Museum might look like had Queen Victoria chosen to live there.' The magazine continued: 'The visitor is ushered down long vistas of tessellated marble floor, past anterooms and beneath arches to a suite crammed with antique marble statuary – miniature Roman heads, fragments of busts, vast, sandaled feet – bronzes, eighteenth-century prints and tapestry-cushioned sofas.' Into which Gianni entered, dressed in a lavender cashmere sweater and charcoal trousers, and remarked of his home: 'I think there is not one moment of art I have forgotten in my house. In each period there is something I like. I'm a collector – but I don't think of it in terms of owning things…as soon as I get money I spend it.'

Vogue continued, 'As he sits there, relaxed but unsmiling, talking commandingly of international fashion and his place in it, the setting and his bearing evoke all the imagery of Italian power…the Roman emperor…the Renaissance prince.' Even the designer's appearance was said to have a classical quality, with numerous reports describing a profile that might have belonged in an ancient bas-relief. His homes, his fashions were all the construction of a powerful fantasy. As *Vogue* reported: 'In family photographs, the Versaces appear in full evening dress on the splendid terraces of Villa Fontanelle on Lake Como, for all the world a haughty, ancient dynasty. In fact, everything they are now has apparently been acquired over the past 12 years…Achieved through Versace corporate family effort, since 1978.'

By the late nineties, Versace's properties included a $7.5 million Manhattan townhouse, his beloved Villa Fontanelle – to which the designer and his partner, Antonio D'Amico, escaped every weekend – and a home on Miami's South Beach, Casa Casuarina. If Lake Como was the Italian *dolce vita* at its most classic and refined, Miami was America at its flashiest and most provocative, a city with a lively gay culture and vivacious mode of dressing that the designer adored. (By his own description, Villa Fontanelle was his 'Proust' property, and Casa Casuarina his 'Batman' abode.) His New York home housed his art collection, including several Picasso, Miro, Léger and Lichtenstein masterpieces, and portraits by the artist Julian Schnabel – who even made a set of beds for the designer, as he revealed in the Versace tome, *The Art of Being You*. 'He'd seen a steel bed I'd made and asked if I'd make one for him…I made it gold because it was a

The mosaic terrace at Versace's South Beach home in Miami. He told Vogue *that he'd fallen in love with the spirit of the city – 'There are no rules.' Photograph by Bruce Weber.*

bed for a King. The bed situation grew. He wanted five beds – for the house in New York – beds for everybody. He wanted beds for each house. The point is that there was no end to his enthusiasm and his generosity. He wanted everyone in his family to share his pleasure. He wanted Antonio to have a portrait [...] He sent Allegra and Daniel [Donatella's children] and little Antonio, Santo's son, to the studio to be painted. He wanted a portrait of his sister Donatella as a Medusa.'

Versace took his patronage and acquisition of art seriously, as a means of building a world of beautiful things around him, but also with an eye to his legacy. From the beginning of his career, he designed costumes for ballets, operas and theatrical productions, creating body-contoured, vividly coloured garments that could be read right up in the gods. These in turn influenced Versace's mainline collections, not least his print stockings and leggings, developed from dancer's tights. Art was an important source of inspiration, and his work frequently made direct reference to artists such as Gustav Klimt, Alexander Calder and Roy Lichtenstein. In *The New York Times*, Ingrid Sischy recalled a dinner at which Versace sat with Madonna and the rapper Tupac Shakur: 'But the person he left with at two in the morning was Philip Taaffe, because he wanted to [...] look at this artist's studio.'

Versace's harlequin-sequinned leggings were a design experiment developed out of his work costuming ballet and opera productions. Photograph by Arthur Elgort.

Overleaf *Stephanie Seymour wears a striking print shirt and leggings (left), conveying the easy elegance of an off-duty dancer. Photograph by Sante D'Orazio Janet Jackson photographed by Herb Ritts for* Vogue *in a jewelled portrait bolero jacket (right). Versace's clothes, in their exclamatory, audacious designs, conveyed the essence of celebrity.*

The designer used his homes as a means to sell the Versace lifestyle, for entertaining actors and pop stars at dinners the journalist Henry Porter described as 'wowing people who needed to be wowed', and as the backdrop to photographs in the brand-building coffee table books published by the label. In Miami, Versace hosted fêtes for Sting, Elton John, Bruce Springsteen, Jack Nicholson, Sylvester Stallone, and Naomi Campbell, who recalled for *Vogue*, 'If there was an evening when he didn't want us to go out, he would transform his house into a nightclub so we could have fun but still stay in with him.' He even redecorated a room for Madonna, in red and gold.

Madonna, who appeared in Versace's publicity campaigns and was a front row regular, wrote of a trip to Villa Fontanelle: 'Every evening at sunset we were served fresh Bellinis, which we sipped under the giant magnolia tree at the edge of the lake. The cook prepared delicious meals, the Sri Lankan servants waited on us with white gloves, and my dog Chiquita was taken for long walks by gorgeous Italian bodyguards with walkie-talkies.' Even she was impressed. 'I was envious of a person who had the courage to live so luxuriously,' she said. 'I felt like a spoilt princess. The Versaces really know how to live.'

'Love's young dreamers', Generation X pin-ups Winona Ryder and Johnny Depp in Vogue, *dressed by Versace and photographed by Herb Ritts.*

Overleaf *Unquestionably the designer's biggest celebrity coup was dressing Princess Diana. Here she is photographed by Patrick Demarchelier wearing a Versace beaded column dress, alongside hairdresser Sam McKnight and make-up artist Mary Greenwell.*

Perhaps Versace's greatest coup was dressing the Princess of Wales. In a 1997 article marking Princess Diana's death, her stylist, the fashion editor Anna Harvey, wrote in *Vogue*: 'After the divorce [from Prince Charles] she was much freer. She wore a lot of Versace – the simple shift dresses and evening columns that he and Catherine Walker were doing for her were probably her most successful look to date.' Diana's hairdresser, Sam McKnight, recalled a *Vogue* shoot for which the magazine had photographed a pale-blue Versace dress on model Christy Turlington. 'We all thought it would look great on the Princess. The next time I saw her I plucked up the courage to show her a Polaroid from the shoot, saying "This would look great on you..." She took one look and said, "But I could never afford that!"'

As Anna Wintour commented of such interactions, 'He was the first to realise the value of the celebrity in the front row, and the value of the supermodel, and put fashion on an international media platform. He relished media attention and masterminded it, and everybody followed in his footsteps.' In a way that was to become standard practice in the fashion industry, Versace cultivated celebrity relationships, finding particular affinity with musicians, including George Michael, David Bowie, Prince and Elton John. The latter became a close friend of the family; Elton was godfather to Donatella's daughter, Allegra, while Donatella's son, Daniel, was named after the Elton John track.

Lots of love Sam,
from Diana x. 1991.

‘SHE WORE A LOT OF VERSACE … PROBABLY HER MOST SUCCESSFUL LOOK.’

VOGUE

When Bono was photographed with Christy Turlington on the cover of a 1992 issue of *Vogue*, what else would he wear but Versace leather jeans? By fusing the worlds of style and music, Versace created a new model for the industry where fashion was no longer the preserve of the moneyed elite, but the domain of the MTV generation.

Versace made wedding outfits for Sting and Trudie Styler, and a going-away outfit for Elizabeth Taylor after her marriage to Larry Fortensky. He dressed Jon Bon Jovi and cast him in an advertising campaign, photographed by Avedon wearing a smile and not much else. Mario Testino said, 'Stars loved wearing his clothes, because for some of them, putting on a Versace was the first time they *felt* like stars.' Despite the vast expense involved in such affiliations, not least the first class flights, the best suites at the best hotels, free clothes and lavish gifts, the effort and outlay were essential to the image and success of the house. It was not without sacrifice, however. As Donatella recalled of meeting Elizabeth Taylor, 'My brother collected vintage jewellery and I was wearing a ring that he'd given me – Elizabeth said in this extraordinary breathy voice: "Darling I love your ring, may I try it?" And she didn't give it back! She put it on and breathed, "Oh darling thank you, you didn't have to do that!" But I hadn't!' The brand's association with fame and money meant the name Versace was haloed with a most seductive glamour: everyone wanted a piece of it, even Elizabeth Taylor.

Rock chic: Christy Turlington shares the Vogue cover with Bono in, of course, leather jeans by Gianni Versace. Photograph by Andrew Macpherson.

'I've always said that I would like to mix rock and simplicity,' said the designer, 'because this is fashion, they're the extremes, chic and shock. That's why Lady Diana and Madonna – two of the most important women of the moment – wear Versace and I think I'm satisfied by this.' The solicitation and upkeep of such relationships were Donatella's area of responsibility at Versace, a role that suited her extroverted character and appetites. Hedonism, both notional and real, was fundamental to the Versace brand. Yet, Gianni was a self-confessed homebody who drank infrequently and spurned drugs, and preferred to get an early night than indulge in the all-night bacchanalias that were Donatella's distinctive style. As *Vogue* wrote of

VOGUE
DEC
£2·50
On the road with
U2
Betty Boo
Michael Hutchence
Donna Karan
Lenny Kravitz
Vanessa Paradis
Karl Lagerfeld
Helen Mirren
Shakespears Sister
rock
FAME
fashion

a post-show party in Milan, 'the joke was that while everyone made small talk and swivelled their eyes ferociously around the room in search of Versace, he had long since vanished to have dinner in a quiet restaurant.' Donatella told the magazine in 2003, 'Gianni found his success very stressful. If we had a party, he always wanted to go to bed at 11.30pm and I'd have to tell him it wasn't allowed.'

Under Donatella's influence, as Ariel Levy reported in *New York* magazine, 'Versace meant whatever you wanted, whenever you wanted it.' Her hospitality was jaw-dropping and tales of her grandiose spending were legend. When she stayed at the Ritz she had her own florist transported from Milan, and once, in the company of Naomi Campbell, she reportedly flew in a hairdresser to tend to the pair's hair extensions. Yet she was, as *Vogue* attested, 'always excellent company', with a kindness and vulnerability behind 'that hard undentable Versace vision of glamour'. A vision that was highly useful to the brand. As Deborah Ball wrote of Donatella, 'The more the rumour spread about the wild parties she threw – with the best-looking people, the best drugs, and the best music – the hotter his brand became. Gianni had long relied on her to add louche glamour to his image, with her blaze of diamonds, candy-gloss hair and poured-on dresses.' As Donatella told Ball, 'I came back and gave him information he wouldn't have had if it weren't for my lifestyle…I was his eyes.'

Perhaps chief amongst her contributions was the masterminding of Versace's million-dollar publicity campaigns, photographed by Bruce Weber, Helmut Newton, Mario Testino, Herb Ritts and, most famously, Avedon, whose pictures, shot against a grey background, articulated a camp and vampy sexuality that was easily decipherable. The label's campaigns were headline-makers, literally so when the house shrewdly offered them to newspapers, pre-release, to be used as editorial coverage – marketing images converted into front-page news, a very Versace innovation.

Playing up to her camp image, Donatella is photographed by Marc Hom for Vogue *in a tank dress with asymmetric hem, trailing male models.*

Overleaf *Kate Moss in Atelier Versace, photographed by Richard Avedon for Versace's advertising campaign (left). From 1979 onwards, the photographer produced the marketing images that delivered a definitive notion of Versace glamour. Moss in Versace's strapless chain-mail mini (right), photographed by Tom Munro for a* Vogue *cover in 1997.*

Versace was life and art with the volume turned up. It was impossible not to have fun while wearing his designs. Here, two glamorous Oroton minidresses hit the floor. Photograph by Dewey Nicks.

Overleaf *Gianni, Donatella and Gianni's beloved niece and heir, Allegra, photographed by Bruce Weber. Paeans to the Versaces – family as marketing strategy – were ubiquitous in the nineties.*

Similarly, the label's glorifying publications – titles like *Rock and Royalty*, *South Beach Stories* – sold the Versace dream to the wider public and weren't afraid to shock. One arresting layout in *Rock and Royalty* positioned the Duke and Duchess of Windsor opposite a full-frontal shot of a naked male model, wrapped in a Versace quilt. Featuring alongside such bold images, and without any apparent sense of disjunct, were glossy photographs of Versace *en famille*, the designer with his beloved niece and nephew. These photographic paeans to the Versace clan – family as marketing strategy – were as ubiquitous as the designer's silk print shirts in the nineties, causing the Italian press to dub the Versace tribe '*ipermediatizzati*', or hyper-media-ised.

Reality did not always match the fantasy. In the mid-nineties, Versace was diagnosed with a rare form of ear cancer, and Donatella was in the grip of a cocaine habit. Versace's illness created tension and rivalry between the siblings as Donatella took on the role of co-designer at her brother's house. For six months before the designer's death, the pair did not speak – 'It was war', Versace acknowledged in 1996 – but were reconciled before his murder. The arguments were nothing new. As *Vogue* asserted, 'theatrical, Italian family feuds between Donatella and Gianni' were a matter of course at the house of Versace. As Paul Beck confided to *Vanity Fair*, 'I thought somebody was going to kill someone. I had to leave the room. And the argument would be over something like where to put the sweaters in the new boutique on Via Montenapoleone.'

In early 1997 Versace was declared cured. His illness had given him a renewed respect for his work, family and life, as the designer voiced to *The New Yorker*: 'I know now that everything passes, that one day I am going to die, as everyone else dies. That every success transforms itself into something that ends. That's to say, I don't have illusions – I'm happy to live, I live intensely, and I don't have regrets.' His words were a foreshadowing. As Donatella told *New York* magazine: 'We celebrated, we drink champagne and everything. Six months later he was killed.'

‘THERE WAS NO END TO HIS ENTHUSIASM AND HIS GENEROSITY. HE WANTED EVERYONE IN HIS FAMILY TO SHARE HIS PLEASURE.’

JULIAN SCHNABEL

'YOU WILL FIND ME IN MY WORK.'

GIANNI VERSACE

MURDER AND LEGACY

Versace's final couture collection was presented at the Ritz in July 1997. The models – including English girls Stella Tennant, Erin O' Connor and Karen Elson, the *jolies laides* championed by Donatella – wore heavy black eye make-up, red lips and leather headbands. Set to an insistent electronic rhythm rather than the usual upbeat pop soundtrack, the presentation was – for the house of Versace, at least – demonstrably sober in tone, with sharply tailored daywear and minimal glitz. Still, this was Versace. The collection remained vitally, visibly *him*, comprising short skirts, acreages of flesh and an up-scaled vision of the designer's ideas in which he manipulated his house signatures – eighties' shoulder pads, for instance, were articulated as padded, sculptural forms – in gestures that proved how far he had come and spoke of an exciting future for the brand. No more so than in the climactic appearance of Naomi Campbell, dressed as a bride in a silvery chain-mail mini-sheath, beaded with Byzantine crosses that glanced and glittered beneath the lights. This was Versace style distilled: art-historical reference, tactile draping, sensual cut and a fabric that was Gianni's own technical invention – not to mention the means of its showcasing, to extraordinary allure, by a supermodel.

At the finale of his autumn/winter 1997 Atelier Versace show, the designer kisses Naomi Campbell, dressed as a bride in a silvery chain-mail mini-sheath, beaded with Byzantine crosses.

Overleaf *The bare essentials of dressing up: Shalom Harlow wears Atelier Versace's silver slingbacks (left). Photograph by Nick Knight. Photographed in Paolo Roversi's distinctive chiaroscuro palette, Amber Valletta wears Atelier Versace's modern interpretation of the slip dress in metallic mesh and black lace (right).*

A few weeks later, on the morning of 15 July 1997, the 50-year-old Versace left his Miami mansion to buy magazines. On his return, the designer was shot twice at point-blank range. By 9.20am, Gianni Versace was declared dead. His killer was 27-year-old Andrew Cunanan, a character known to Miami's gay scene and for whom Versace had become an object of obsession. (The pair were unknown to each other.) A suspect in four other homicides, Cunanan was already the subject of a nationwide manhunt. The day after Versace's funeral, he was discovered hiding on a houseboat. Cunanan had committed suicide. He left no explanation as to why he murdered the designer.

News of Gianni's death spread around the world. Television reports featured an incongruent mix of footage, contrasting the chaos unfolding at Casa Casuarina with images of supermodels on the Versace catwalk.

Italian newspaper *La Repubblica* declared: 'He was killed like a prince laid low in his own blood, with one hand outstretched towards his oil paintings, his tapestries, his gold.' *Time*'s Miami bureau chief, Tammerlin Drummond, described the surreal scene at the gates of the designer's villa: 'There was a squirrel on a leash perched atop a man's head. A dachshund wearing a necklace pranced about, and models were everywhere, mugging for the cameras.'

The rumours were rampant – was Cunanan a jealous boyfriend? Was the murder a mafia assassination? Stories of a connection to organised crime had swirled around the Versace family since the label's inception. (False and unfounded.) Meanwhile, the fashion world mourned. As Cathy Horyn later wrote in *The New York Times*, 'Try to imagine your wardrobe without the jolt of a print, the vitality of a stiletto, the glamorous bric-a-brac of chains and doodads. This was Versace's doing. His influence melted and spread far beyond the sexual heat of his runway.' Tributes flooded in from his celebrity friends, most of whom attended the designer's memorial mass on 22 July at Milan's Duomo, where the family had been given special dispensation to hold the service. In its scale and grandeur, it resembled a state funeral. Two thousand attended, with thousands more lining the surrounding streets, eager to catch sight of such notables as Julian Schnabel, Elton John and, of course, Princess Diana – whose own funeral was only weeks away.

In the cathedral, supermodels and factory workers mixed with Versace's design contemporaries: Valentino, Gianfranco Ferré, Carla Fendi, Azzedine Alaïa. After standing to sing a psalm with Sting, a weeping Elton John was offered comfort by Princess Diana (the scene captured by a photographer organised and sanctioned by the house). In the windows of Versace boutiques around the world, simple white gowns were placed on mannequins; the busy Via della Spiga, site of Gianni's debut store, was closed for the duration of the memorial mass. Karl Lagerfeld said, 'Of all the designers, he was the one I was closest to and knew best. He made the dream of his youth out of his life.'

For one of his last sittings for Vogue, *the legendary Horst P. Horst photographs Yasmin Le Bon in sculptural, silhouetted silk taffeta layers by Versace.*

Overleaf *A red wool, loosely tailored look is Versace's reinvention of the power suit for the nineties generation (left). Photograph by Regan Cameron. An ultra-short dungaree dress in patent leather (right), red enough to stop traffic – the very point of a Versace dress. Photograph by Raymond Meier.*

Versace's legacy was a house at the peak of success. The designer had been in negotiations to list the company on the stock market, the next step in the expansion of the all-conquering Versace empire. Its net sales for the year were set to top $1 billion. In 1997 there were 300 Versace boutiques worldwide and thousands of affiliated stores selling licensed products marked with the label's unmistakable insignia. Versace had recovered from cancer and returned to work invigorated. Yet, with his death the future of the house was in sudden, serious jeopardy. How to continue with a label so defined by the personality of its creator? Donatella had proved herself a capable co-designer during Gianni's illness, and though she did not share her brother's far-ranging talent, her work at Versus showed an obvious flair and point of view. But trouble loomed. In May 1997 Santo Versace had been found guilty of bribing rogue tax officials, a conviction which he appealed. (The *Mani Pulite* – 'clean hands' – investigation, as it was known, also accused half a dozen of Versace's fellow designers, including Armani and Gianfranco Ferré. They all freely admitted their guilt and testified to the inspectors' corruption. As Santo told *The New Yorker*, 'They paralyzed us. The only way to get rid of them was to pay them off.')

Through dynamic use of colour, Versace conveyed a sense of freedom in his clothes. Here, a striking yellow silk cocktail dress is taken for a turn in Paris. Photograph by Patrick Demarchelier.

Overleaf *From his earliest years, the designer's work was distinct for its inventive use of texture and technique. A fine silk polka dot camisole is tucked into a matching wrap skirt with flyaway layers (left). Photograph by Albert Watson. An asymmetric swathe of a velvet dress (right) is evidence of the lessons in cut and form Versace absorbed in his mother's atelier. Photograph by Lothar Schmid.*

Added to this was the very real threat to the house posed by Donatella's spending habits and her growing drug dependence. Donatella had always worked in collaboration with Gianni – she was muse, confidante and accomplice, not boss. Cathy Horyn wrote of 'how protected Donatella was by the screen of her brother's fame and talent. She was completely free to dazzle, a living Medusa. I won't say she was innocent – the Versaces were never innocent. But she possessed a fragility and a candour that helped to mediate the more implausible parts of her existence.' But now she was alone. As she later recounted to *New York* magazine, 'He was my best friend. I really loved him. I couldn't find a reason why he was killed.

This was a horrible murder and this company he created, they were looking at me like, "What's she gonna do? The king is dead."' The family quickly released a statement: 'We would like the world to be assured that the indomitable spirit, the amazing vitality and the faith in creativity that makes Gianni Versace so important to everyone is something that we are completely committed to and most capable of continuing.'

It would not be easy, however. Gianni's will contained a revelation: he had made his beloved niece his sole heir. Allegra, an eleven-year-old child, now owned 50% of the company, with the other half divided between Santo and Donatella, a decision that saddled the label with difficulties. A month after the will was disclosed, and in front of an audience that included Miuccia Prada, Karl Lagerfeld and Giorgio Armani, Donatella made her debut as head of the house of Versace. The show was well-received, but Donatella struggled to find her voice as a designer, telling *Vogue* in 1998, 'I'm not enjoying these women's collections yet. It's so strange for me because I always thought they were such fun.'

The comeback queen. Having led the house away from financial ruin after the murder of her brother, Donatella is photographed by Mario Testino, aloft and victorious, in 2006.

Subsequent presentations were criticised for a lack of cohesion, and key stores dropped the label. It took a 2004 intervention – staged by Allegra and Elton John – and a subsequent sojourn in rehab, for Donatella and the label to begin their climb back to success. Versace's art collection and homes – including the Miami and Lake Como properties – were sold to raise capital. And in 2012 the house returned to profit. With Donatella at its head, and stronger than ever, the label is once again a fashion powerhouse, selling the Versace dream to a hungry audience around the world, the brand's unique stamp of luxury on everything from clothing to hotels, to interiors schemes for private jets and helicopters.

The continuing life of a label depends on the strength of its signature elements – the houses of Dior, Chanel and Balenciaga were all able to outlive the death of their namesakes owing to the power of their silhouette and inimitable designs. For Versace, the house codes were

vigorously established, embodied in the Oroton dress, the Medusa logo, a deft way with safety pins, straps and body-conscious tailoring, and a vision of femininity that was thrillingly bold and fearless. Six years after Gianni's death, the designer was memorialised in an exhibition, 'Versace at the V&A'. Touring the show, Donatella said, 'Seeing all these dresses together, I can hardly believe my brother was such a genius.'

Vogue wrote, 'more than most of his contemporaries, Versace challenged northern European/American good taste. Where he came from – Calabria, in Italy's flashy, earthy soul – showing your wealth, your youth, your curves and your tan in a single outfit was the norm. Why else bother to get dressed?' Versace meant clothing for liberated women, and was designed to liberate, too, releasing the wearer from restrictive maxims on good taste, from received notions of femininity, from timidity in personal style, and boring convention. Versace triumphed, according to *Time* magazine, because the designer maintained an unerring sense of what he was selling: 'a fantasy life of opulent sensuality'. The latter was writ large in the gleaming surfaces of the Versace experience – in the peacocks strutting his runways, in his exultant vision of glamour, in his synthesis of the traditional and contemporary, colour and print, baroque and rock 'n' roll. Fashion *à la* Versace was embracing, celebratory, life-affirming and enhancing. As Gianni told *The New Yorker*: 'I am working – I am *screaming* – to take women and men away from taboo. Fashion is not just a piece of fabric. No, no, no. It's an attitude, it's a way to express. It's you.' In life as in his designs, Gianni Versace was never afraid to dazzle.

The Renaissance prince and master of all he surveys. Photographed by Snowdon for Vogue *in his Milan home, the designer is on top of the world. In life as in his designs, Gianni Versace was never afraid to dazzle.*

'He made the dream of his youth out of his life.'

KARL LAGERFELD

Index

Page numbers in *italic* refer to illustrations

References

Versace by Richard Martin, Thames and Hudson, 1997

The Art and Craft of Gianni Versace by Claire Wilcox, V&A Publications, 2002

Versace: Signatures by Gianni Versace, Abbeville Press, 1993

House of Versace: The Untold Story of Genius, Murder and Survival by Deborah Ball, Random House, 2011

Versace: The Naked and the Dressed by Richard Avedon, Random House, 1998

Gianni Versace: Fashion's LastEmperor by Lowri Turner, Andre Deutsch, 1997

Gianni Versace by Richard Martin, Getty Program for Art on Film, 1998

Versace by Daniel K Davis, Checkmark Books, 2011

Vanitas: Designs by Gianni Versace and Hamish Bowles, Abbeville Press, 1994

Do Not Disturb by Gianni Versace, Abbeville Press, 1996

Men Without Ties by Gianni Versace, Abbeville Press, 1996

The Art of Being You by Gianni Versace, Abbeville Press, 1998

Rock and Royalty by Gianni Versace, Abbeville press, 1997

Picture References

Author's acknowledgements:
Many thanks to all at British *Vogue*, including Alexandra Shulman, Harriet Wilson, and, particularly, Ben Evans and Brett Croft, and to Jane O'Shea, Sarah Mitchell, Nicola Ellis, Gemma Hayden and the Versace archive and press offices in London and Milan.

Publishing Consultant Jane O'Shea
Creative Director Helen Lewis
Series Editor Sarah Mitchell
Series Designer Nicola Ellis
Designer Gemma Hayden
Production Director Vincent Smith
Production Controllers Sasha Taylor, Emily Noto

For *Vogue*:
Commissioning Editor Harriet Wilson
Picture Researcher Ben Evans

First published in 2015 by
Quadrille Publishing Limited
Pentagon House
52-54 Southwark Street
London SE1 1UN
www.quadrille.co.uk

Quadrille is an imprint of Hardie Grant
www.hardiegrant.com.au

Cataloguing in Publication Data: a catalogue record for this book is available from the British Library.

ISBN 978 184949 553 0

Printed in China